DARK AND EERIE
PIECES
FOR
PIANO

Erebus Society

First published in Great Britain in 2015
Erebus Society

Second Edition

Arrangement by Konstantinos Papatheodorou

ISBN 978-0-9933284-2-8

CONTENTS

Lieder Ohne Worte
Venetianisches Gondellied

Felix Mendelssohn

Op.30, No.6

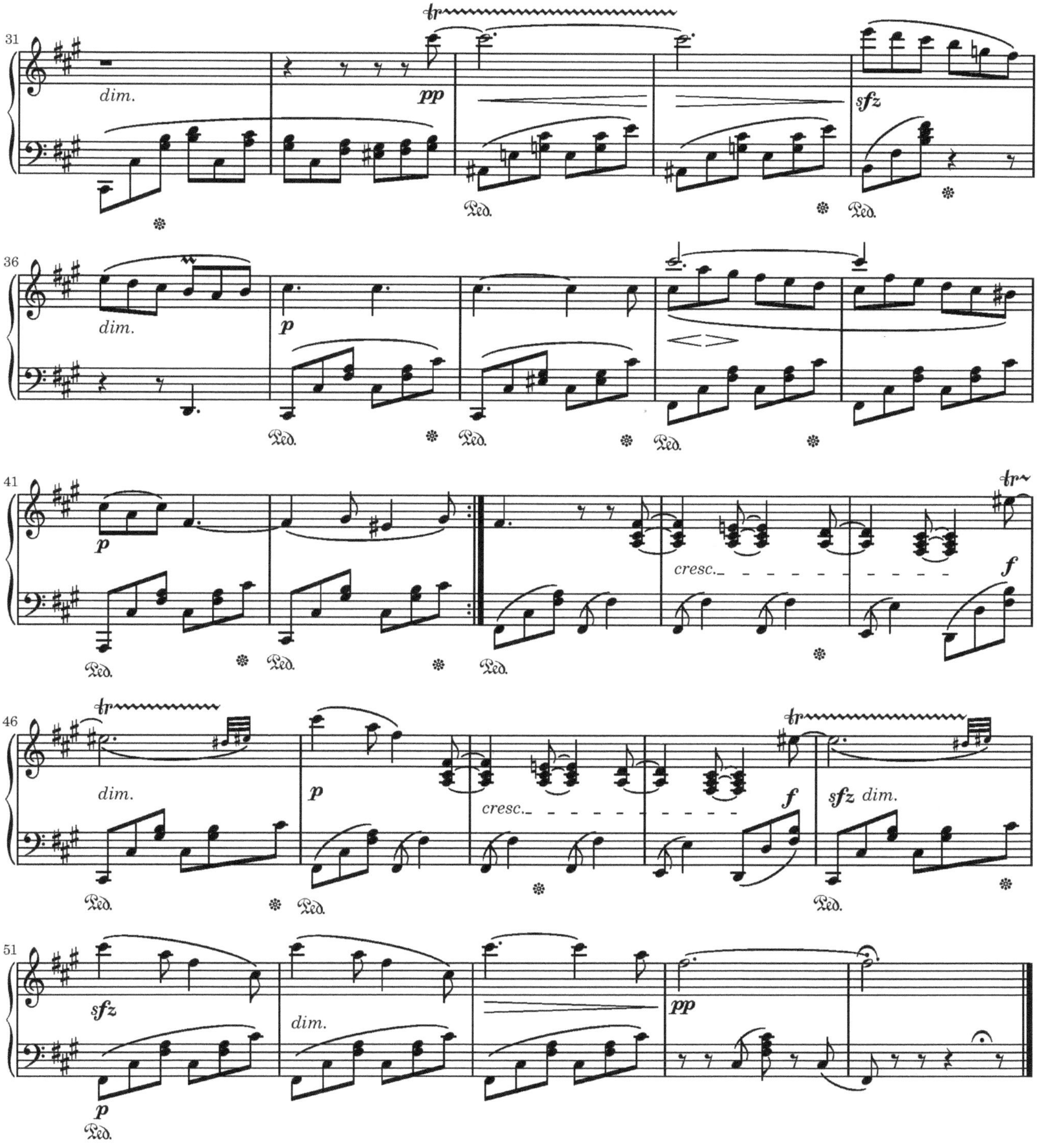

dim.
pp
sfz
dim.
p
cresc.
f
dim.
p
cresc.
f
sfz dim.
sfz
p
dim.
pp

Sonata No.2

Funeral March

Frederic Francois Chopin

Opus 35

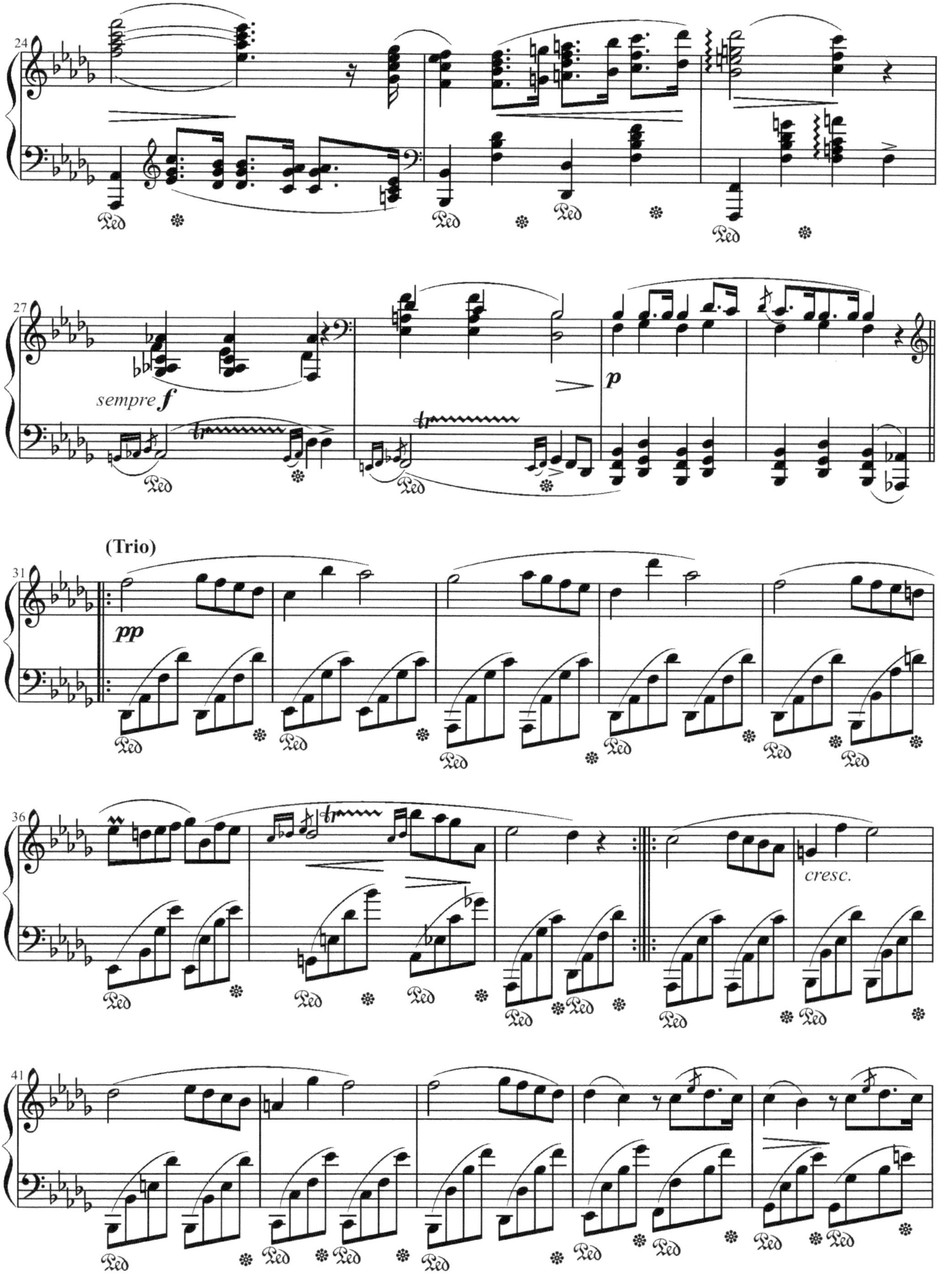

24
27
sempre f
p
(Trio)
31
pp
36
cresc.
41

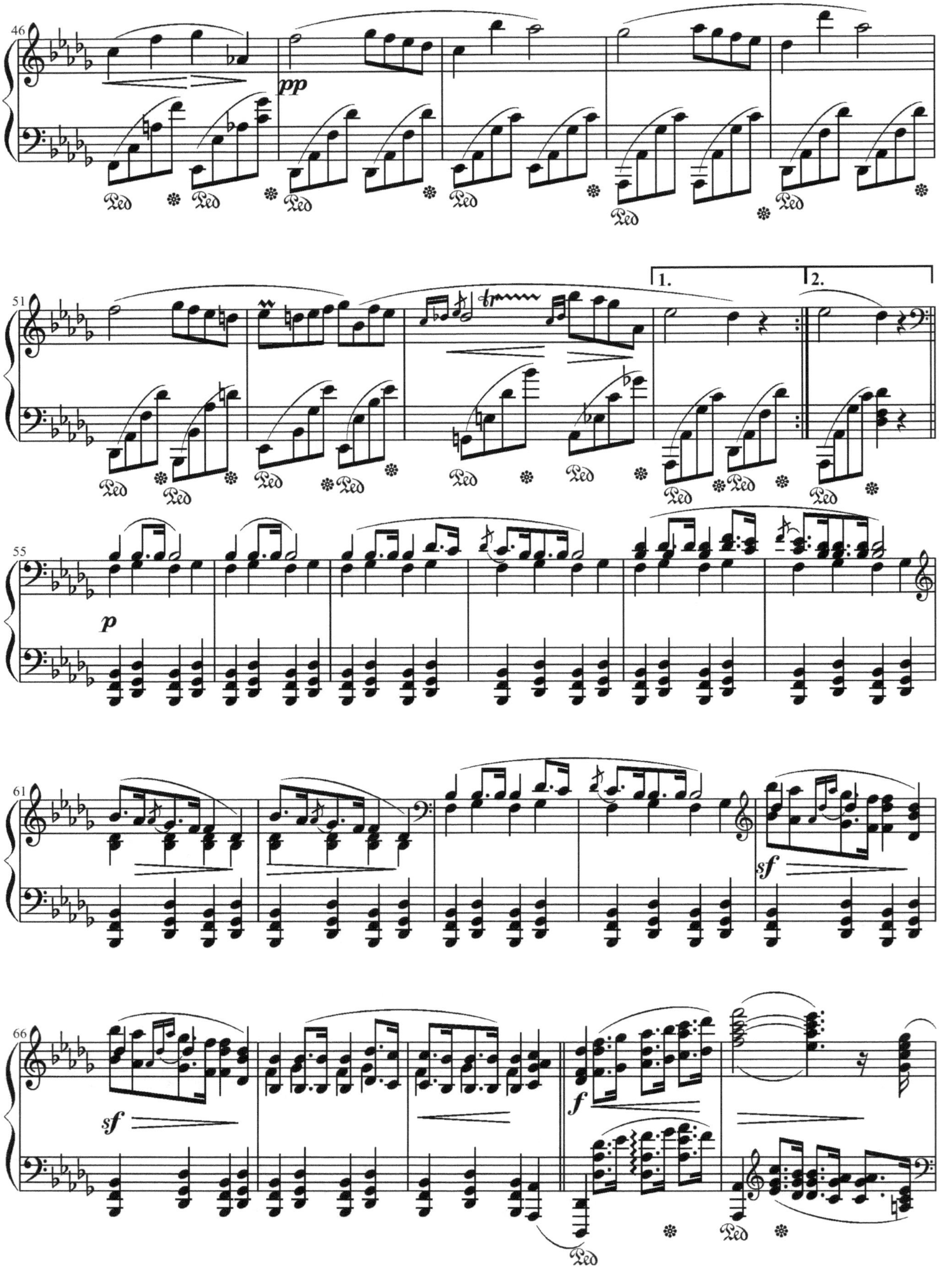
46
pp
Ped
51
1.
2.
55
p
61
sf
66
f

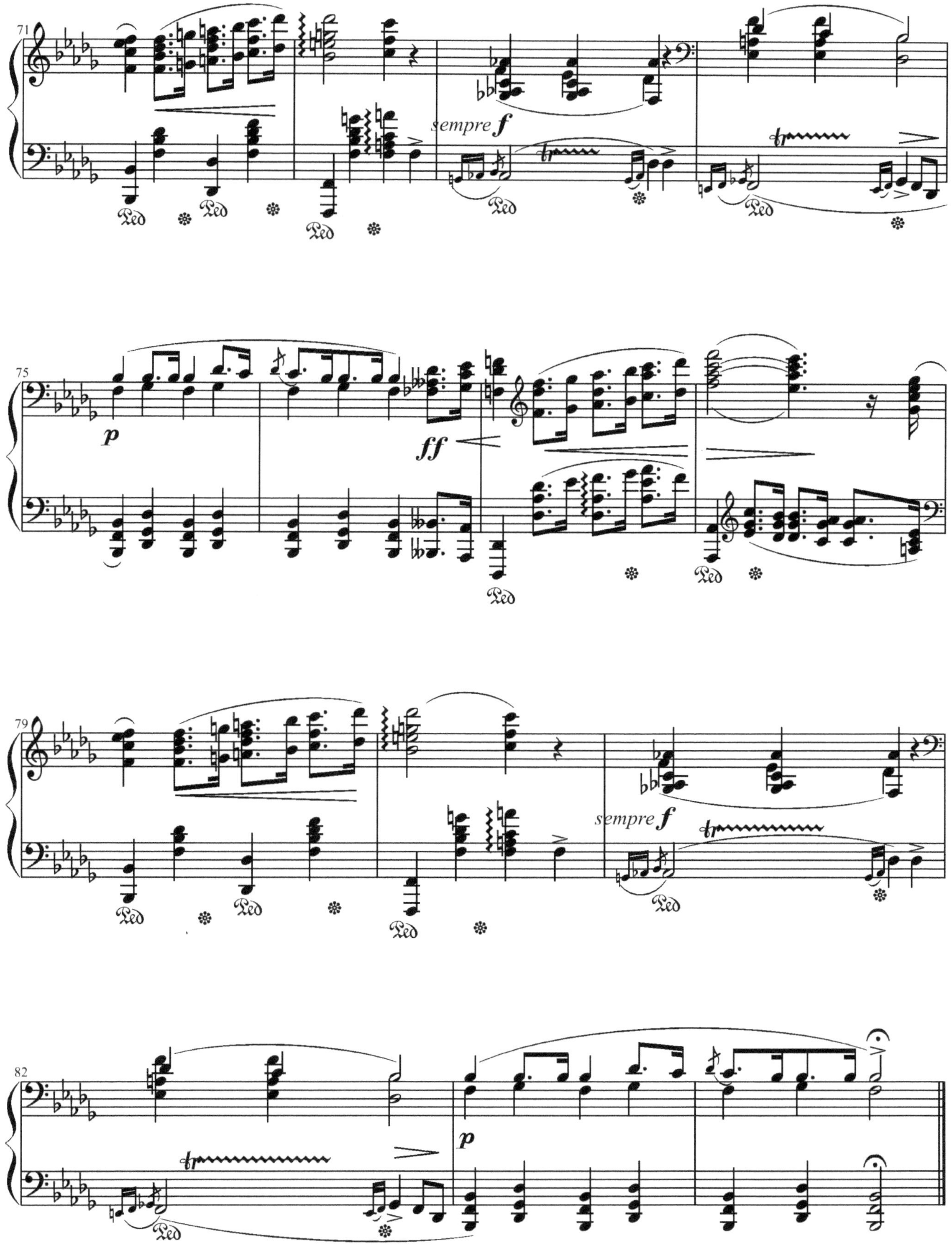
71
sempre f
Ped
75
p
ff
79
sempre f
82
p
tr

Sonata No.14
Moonlight Sonata
1st Movement

Ludwig Van Beethoven

Op.27, No.2

ADAGIO SOSTENUTO

sempre **pp** *e senza sordino*

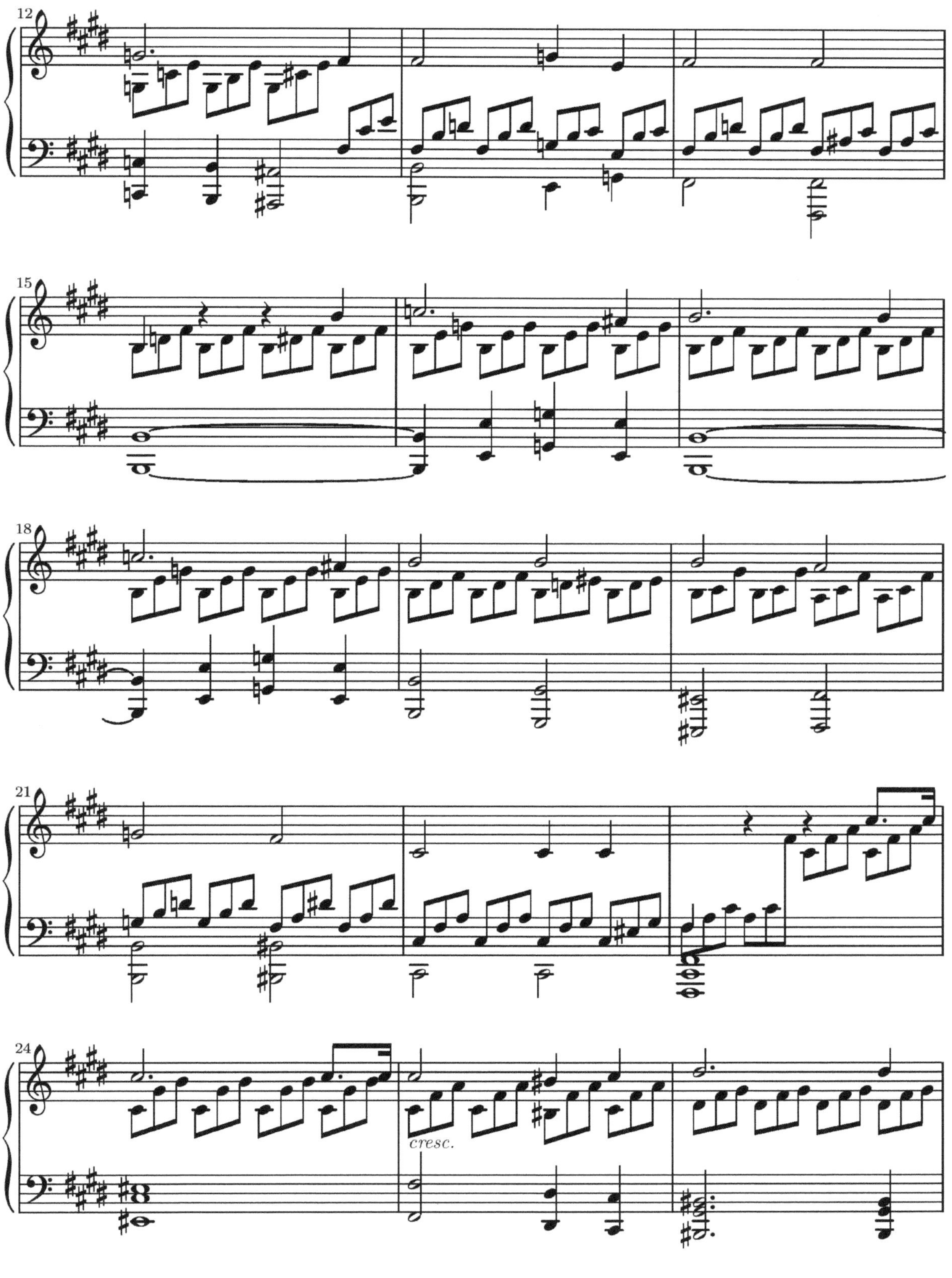

12
15
18
21
24
cresc.

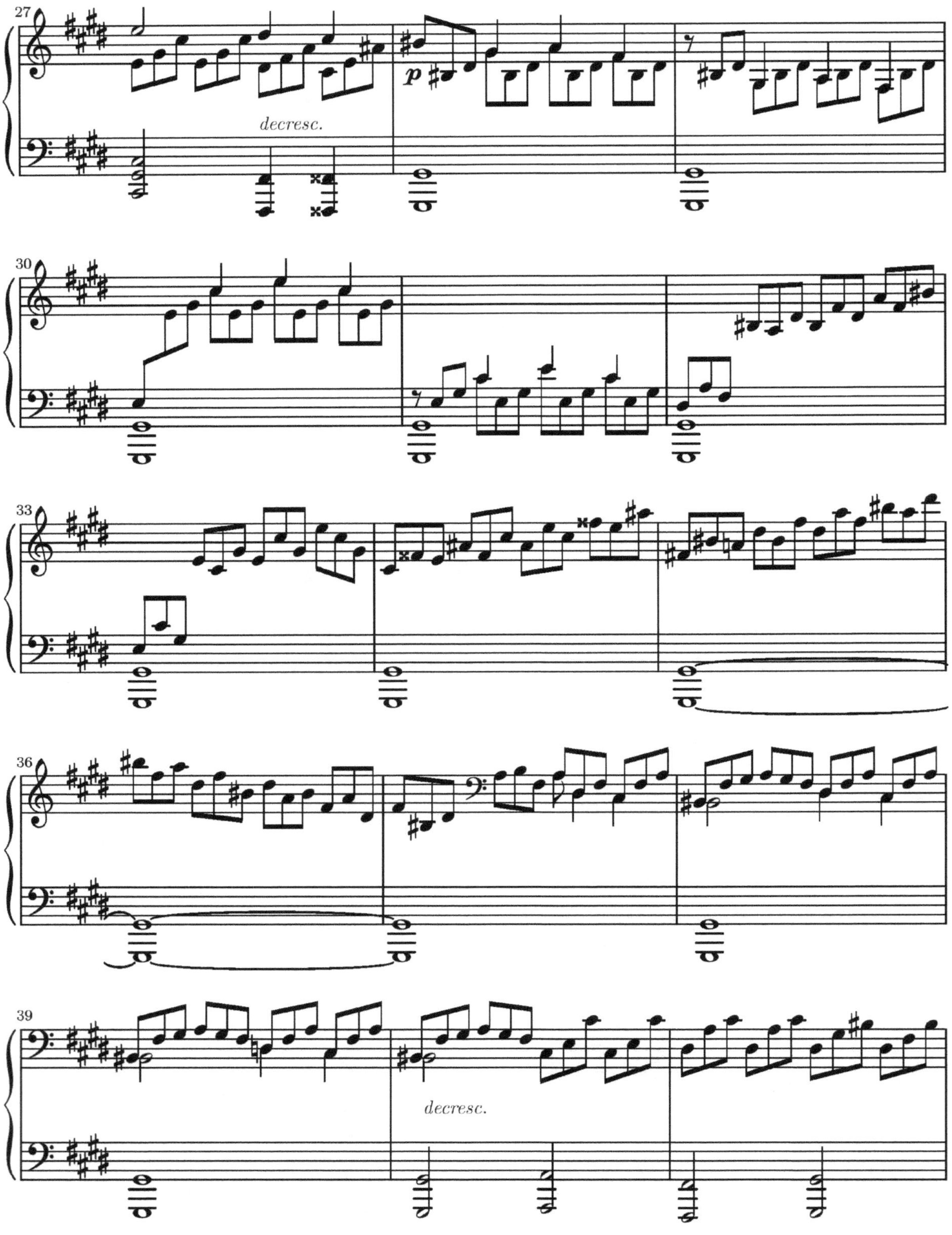

27
p
decresc.
30
33
36
39
decresc.

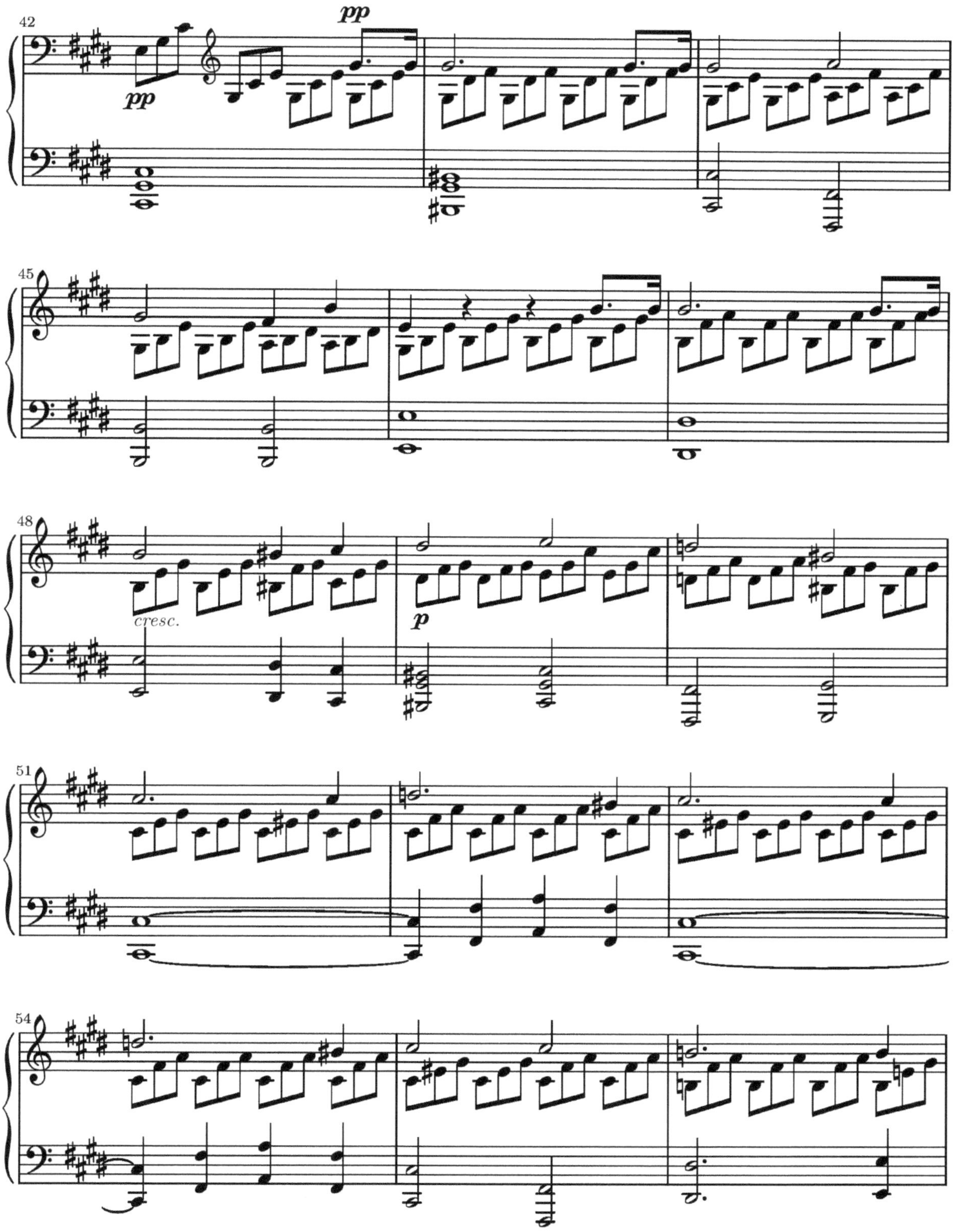
42
pp
pp
45
48
cresc.
p
51
54

attacca subito
il seguente

Requiem in D minor

Lacrimosa

Wolfgang Amadeus Mozart

K.626

La___ cri mo - sa, Di___ es il - la, Qua Re - Sur - Get

Ex Fa - vil - la Ju - di - can - dus Ho - mo Re - us.

La - cri - mo - sa Di - es il - la

11

Qua_____ Re___ sur get Ex_____ Fa - vil - la,

Ju_____ di - can - dus Ho_____ mo Re - us

Hu - ic Er - go Par - ce De - us

Pie Je - su Do - mi - ne.

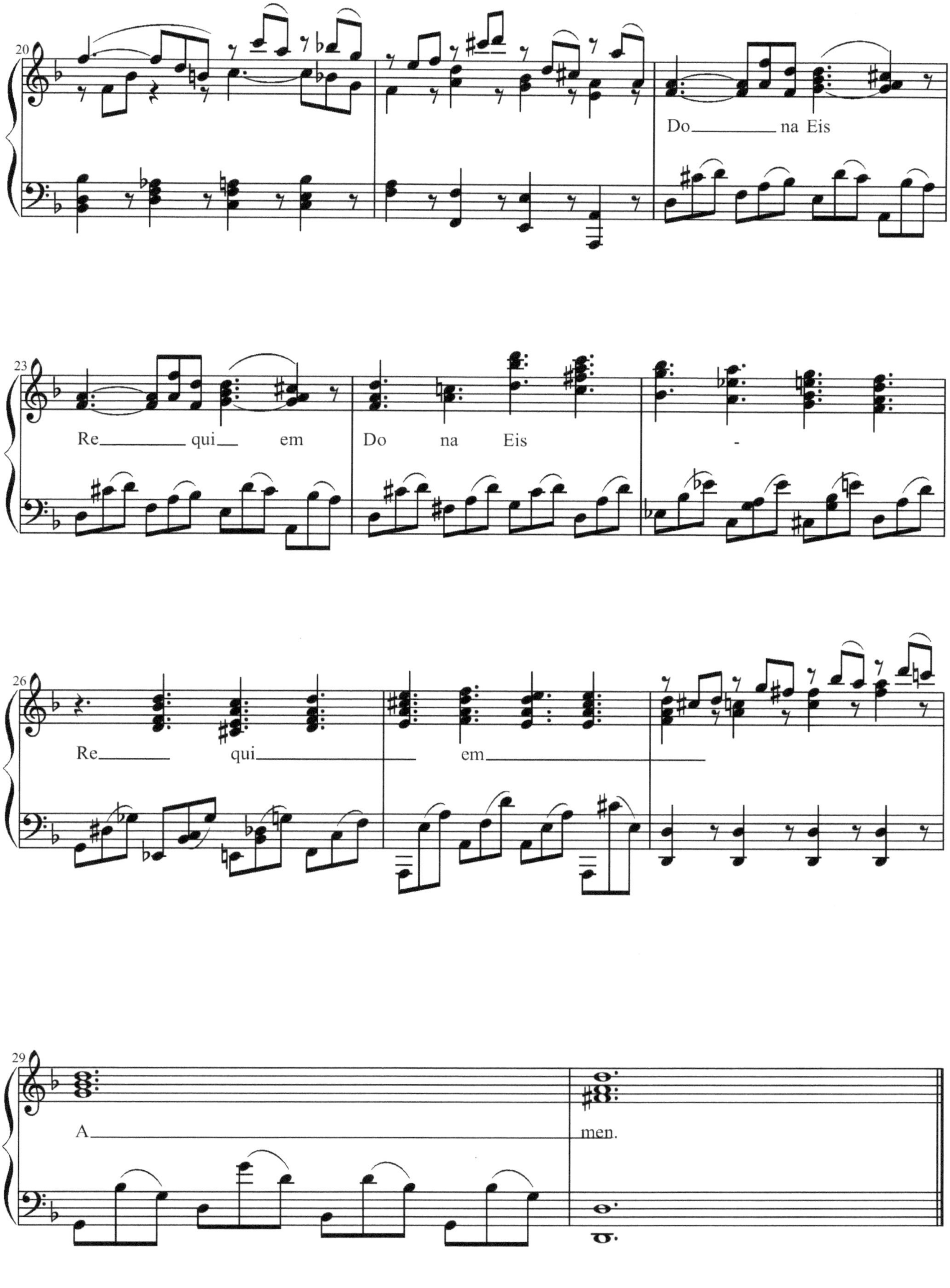
20
Do na Eis
23
Re qui em
Do na Eis
-
26
Re qui em
29
A men.

Sonata No.23

Appassionata

Ludwig Van Beethoven

Op.57

Allegro assai.

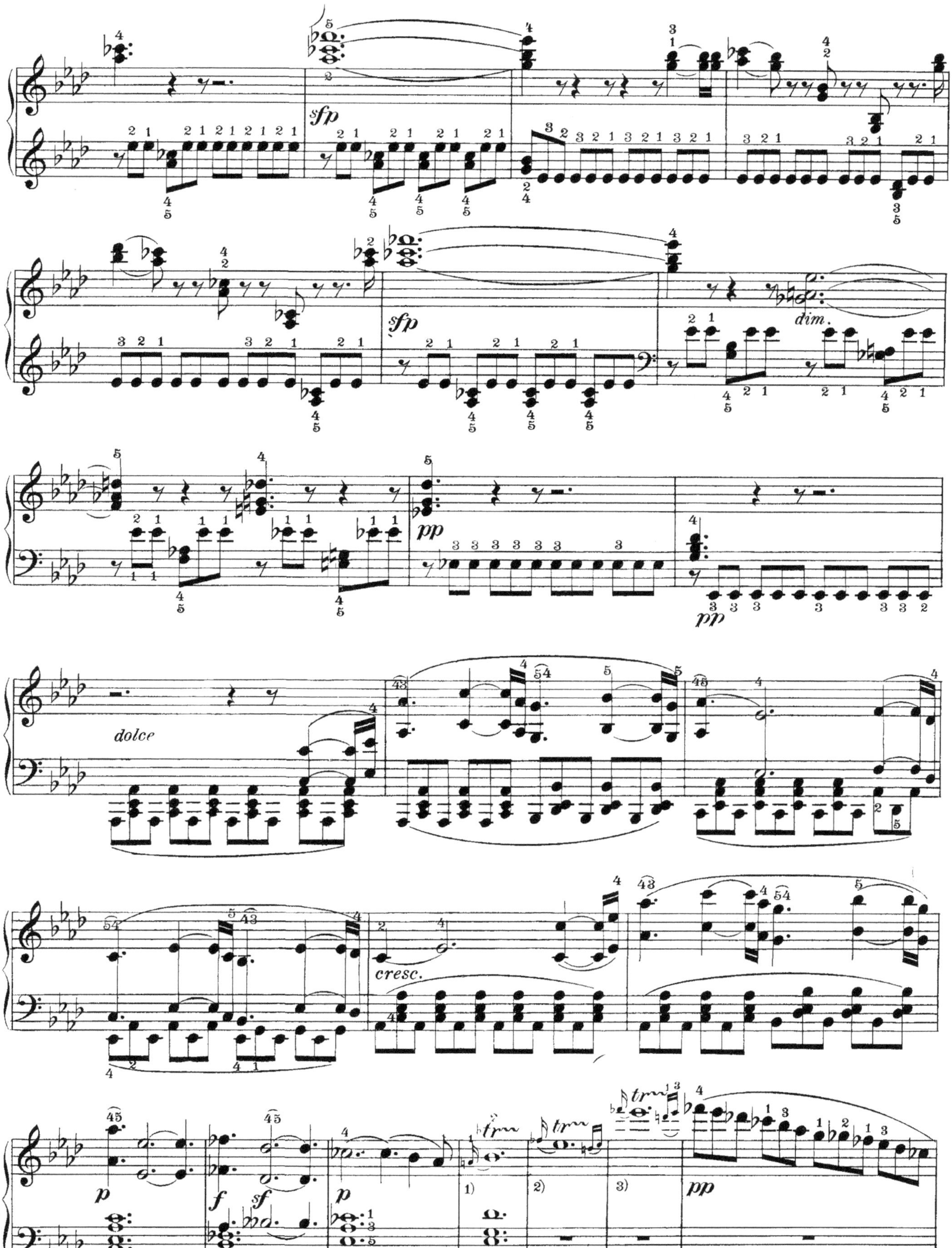
sfp
sfp
dim.
pp
pp
dolce
cresc.
p
f
sf
p
tr
1)
2)
3)
pp

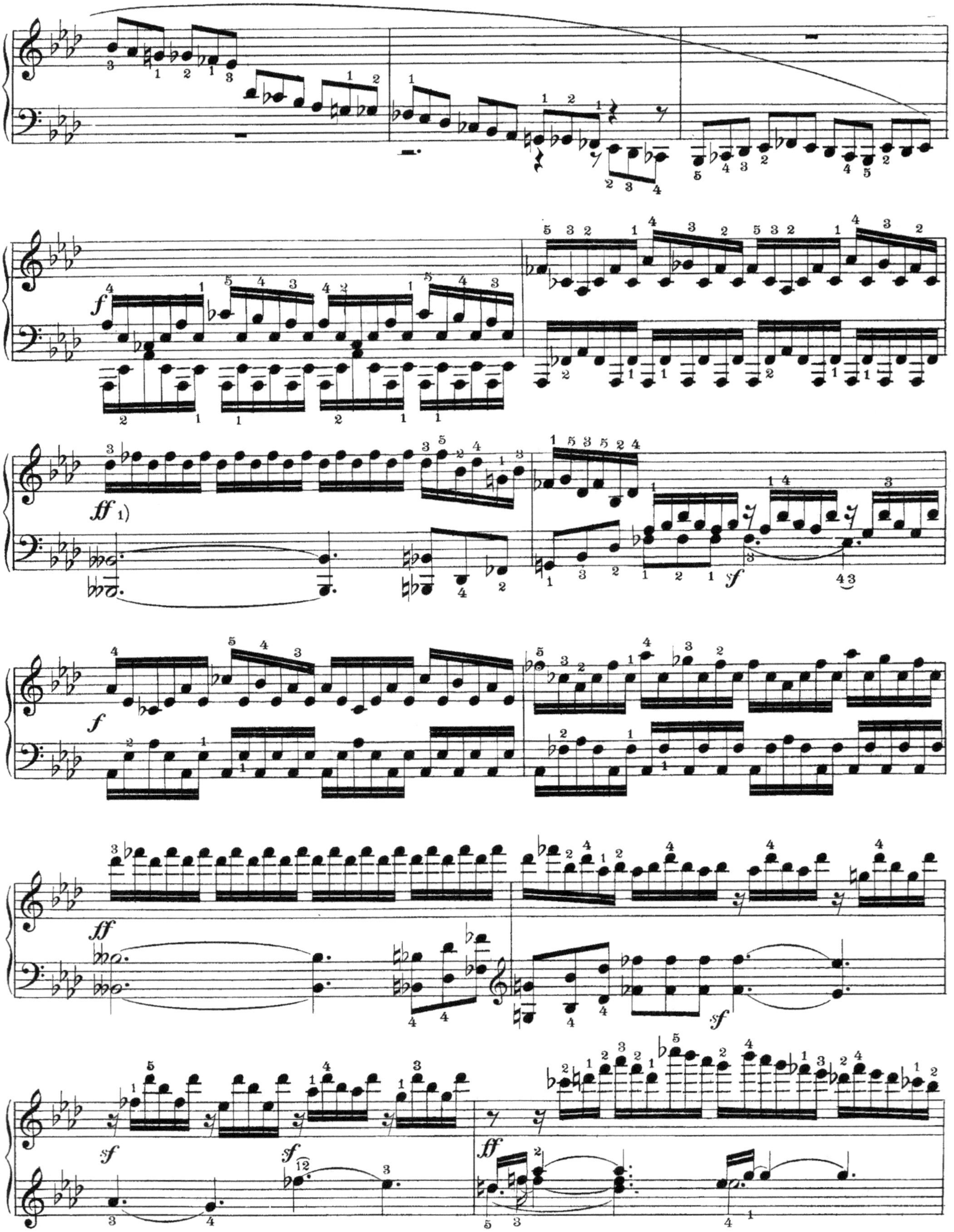
f
ff 1)
sf
f
ff
sf
sf
sf
ff

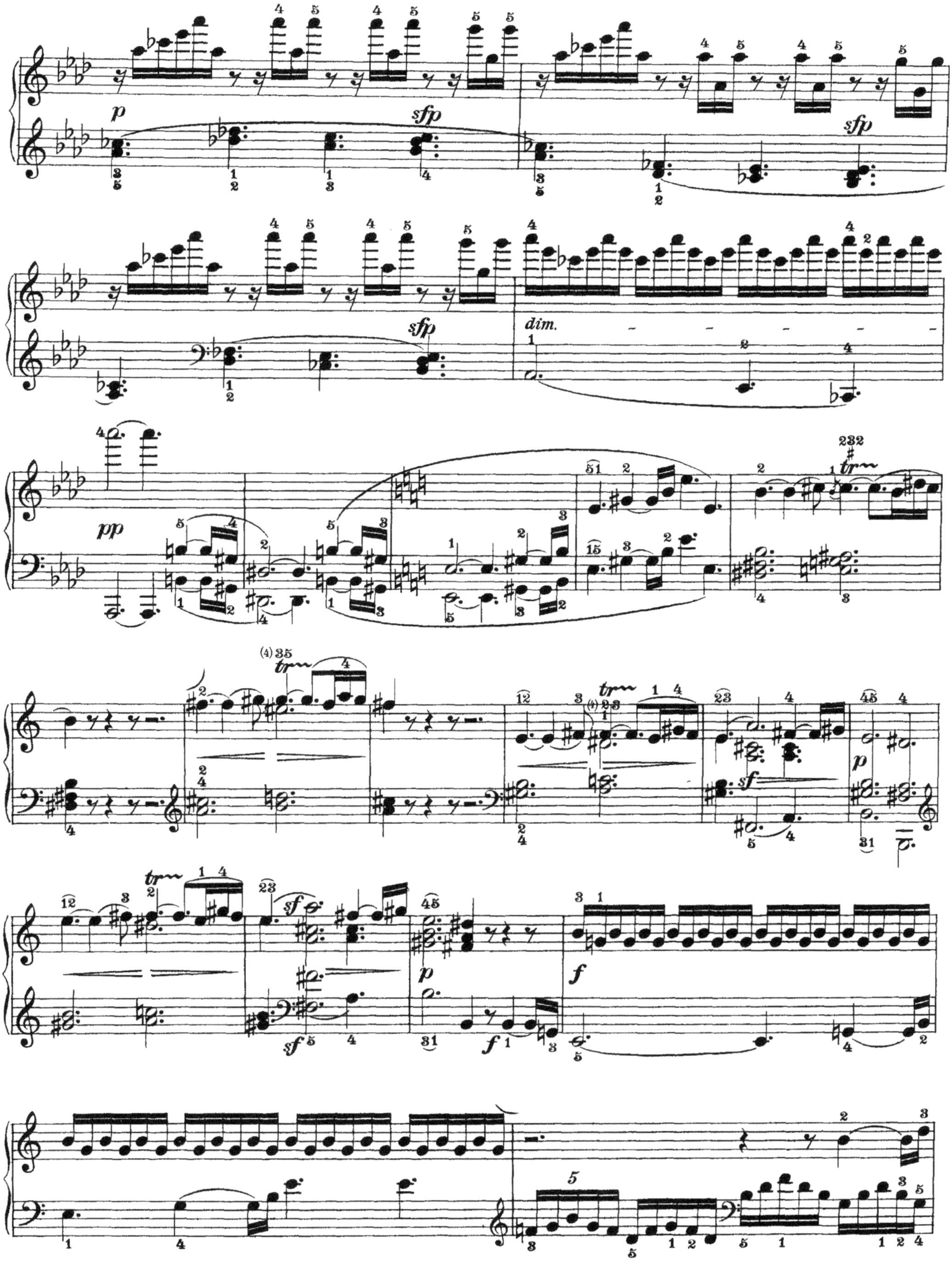
p
sfp
sfp
sfp
dim.
pp
tr
sf
p
sf
p
f
f

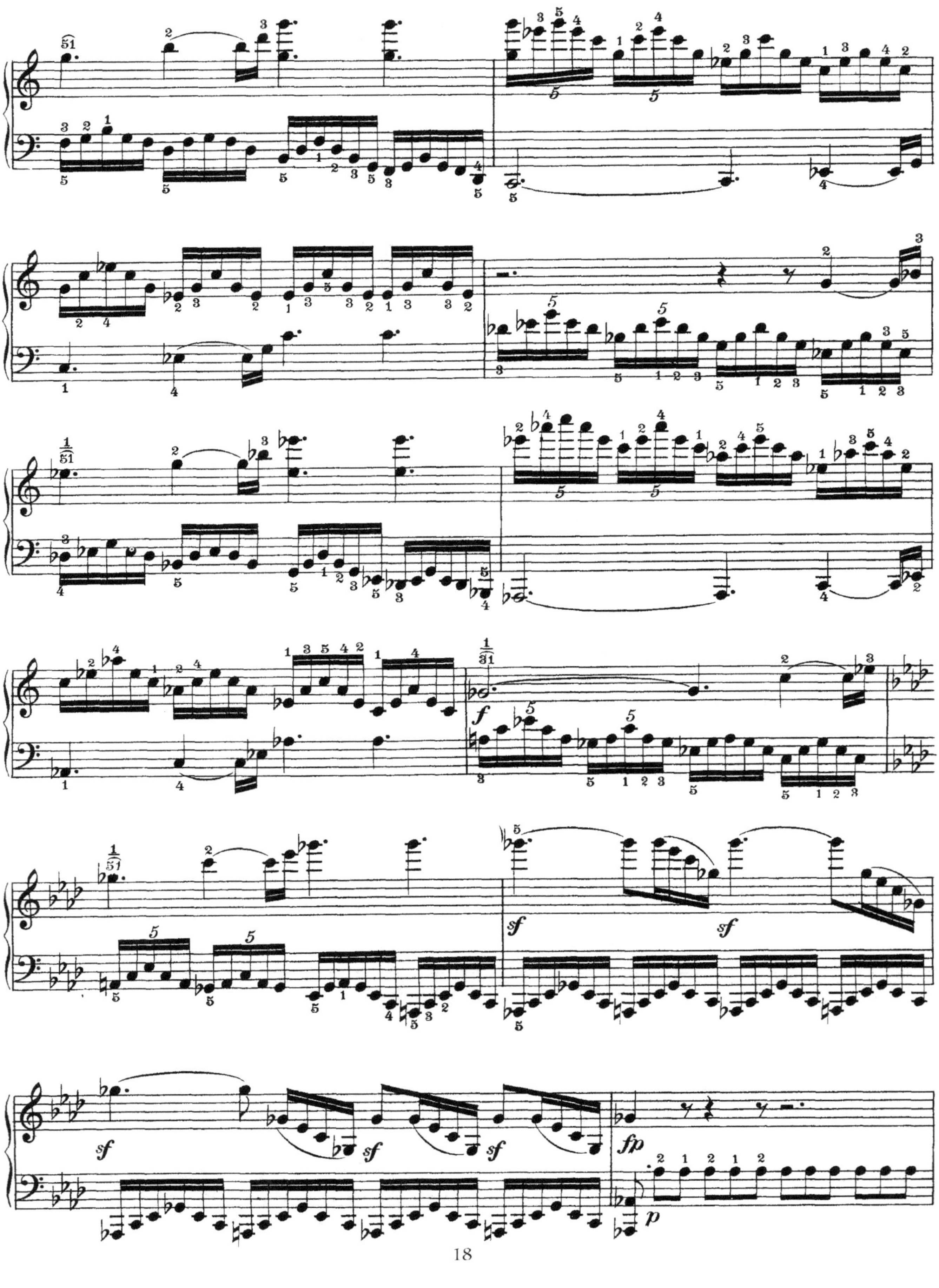
f
sf
sf
sf
sf
sf
fp
p

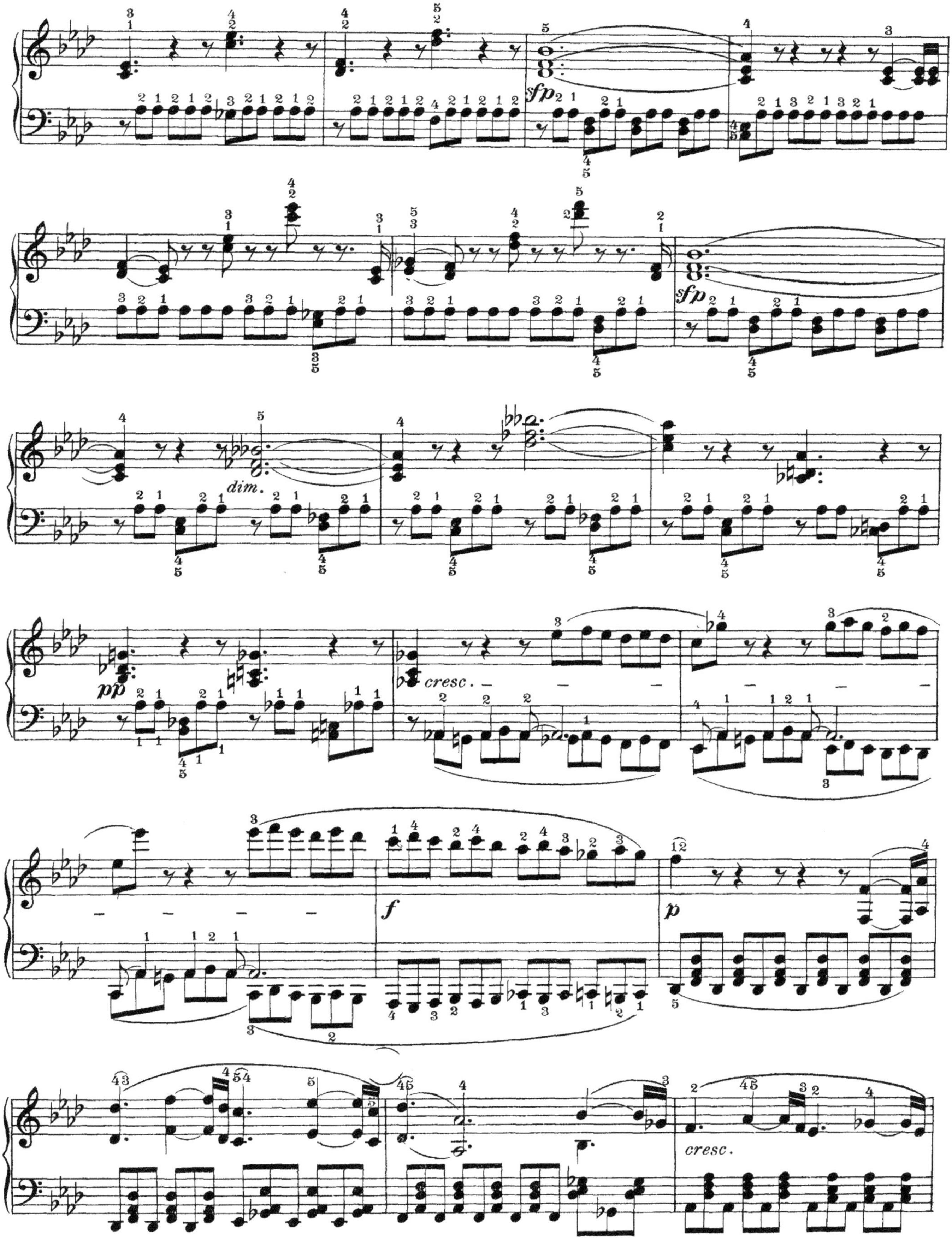
sfp
sfp
dim.
pp
cresc.
f
p
cresc.

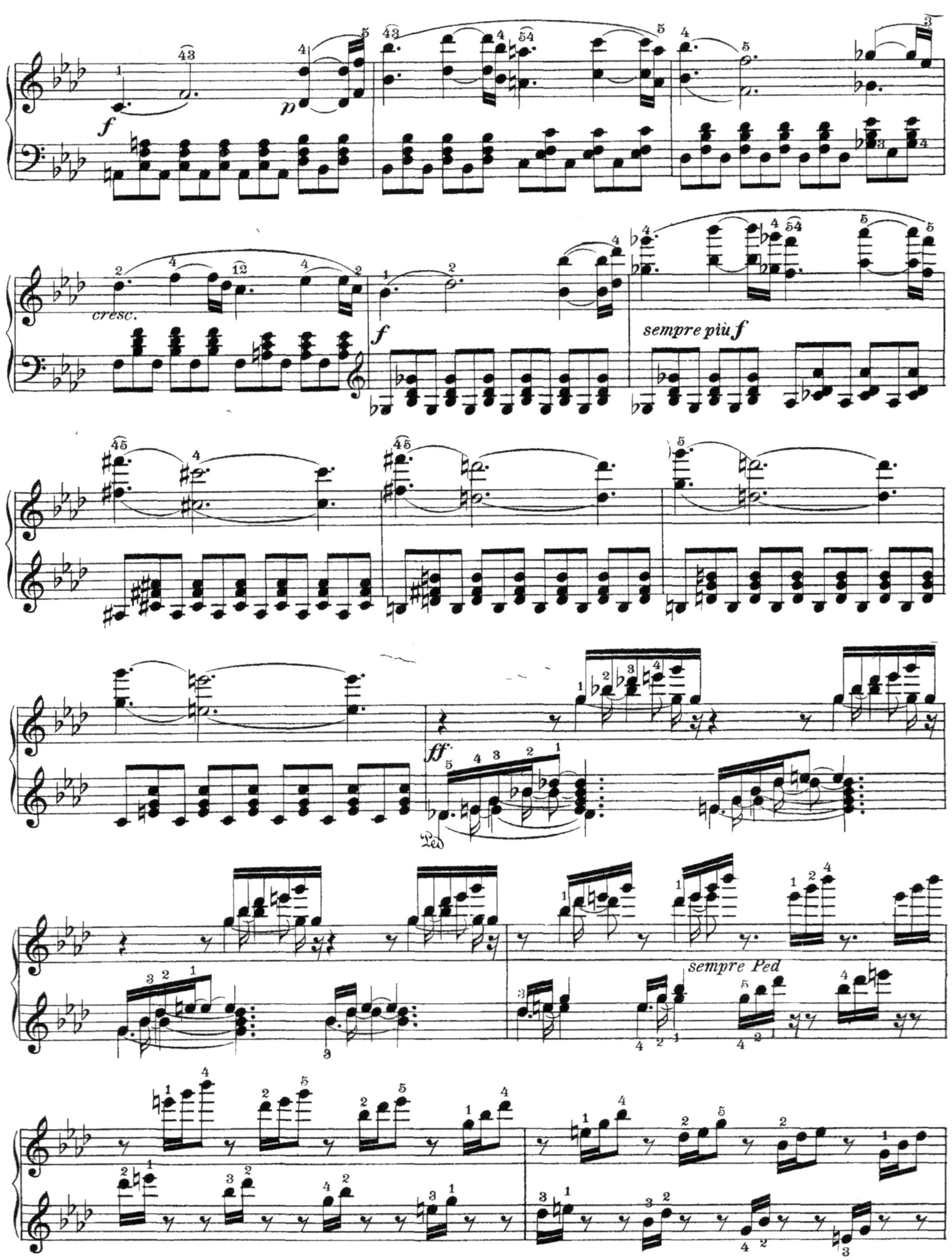
f
p
cresc.
f
sempre più f
ff
Ped
sempre Ped

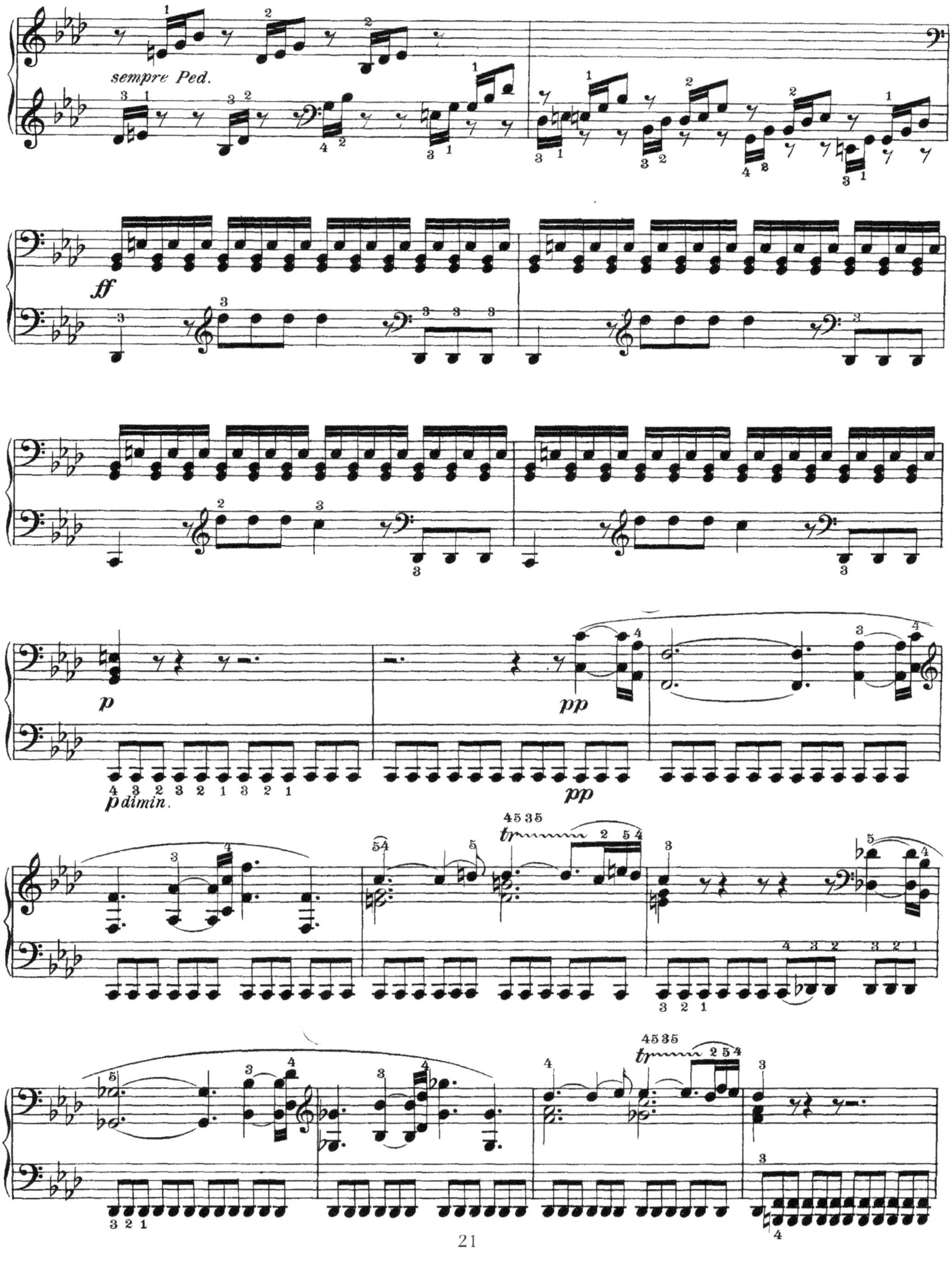
sempre Ped.
ff
p
pp
p dimin.
pp
tr
tr

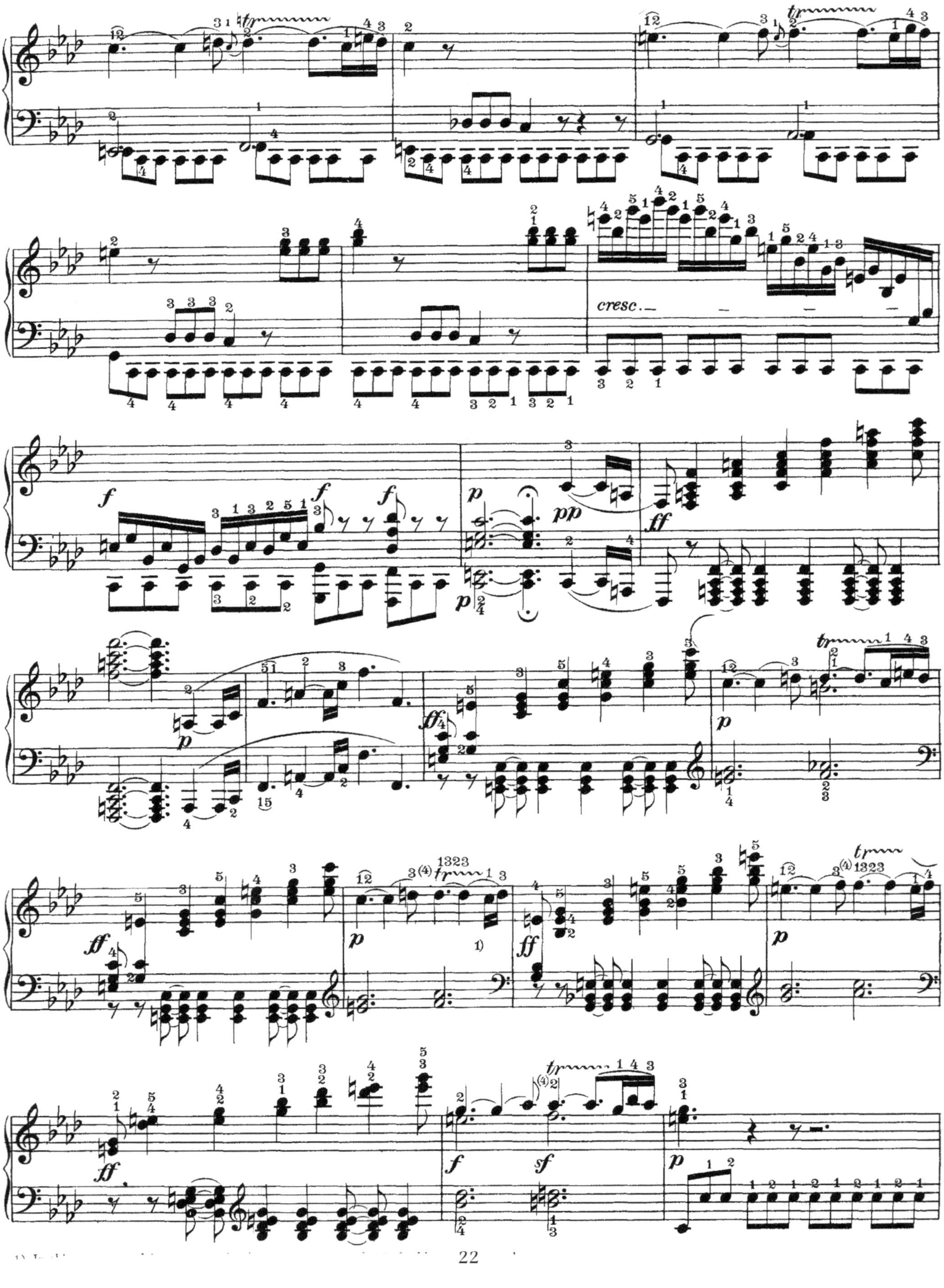
cresc.
f
p
pp
ff
sf

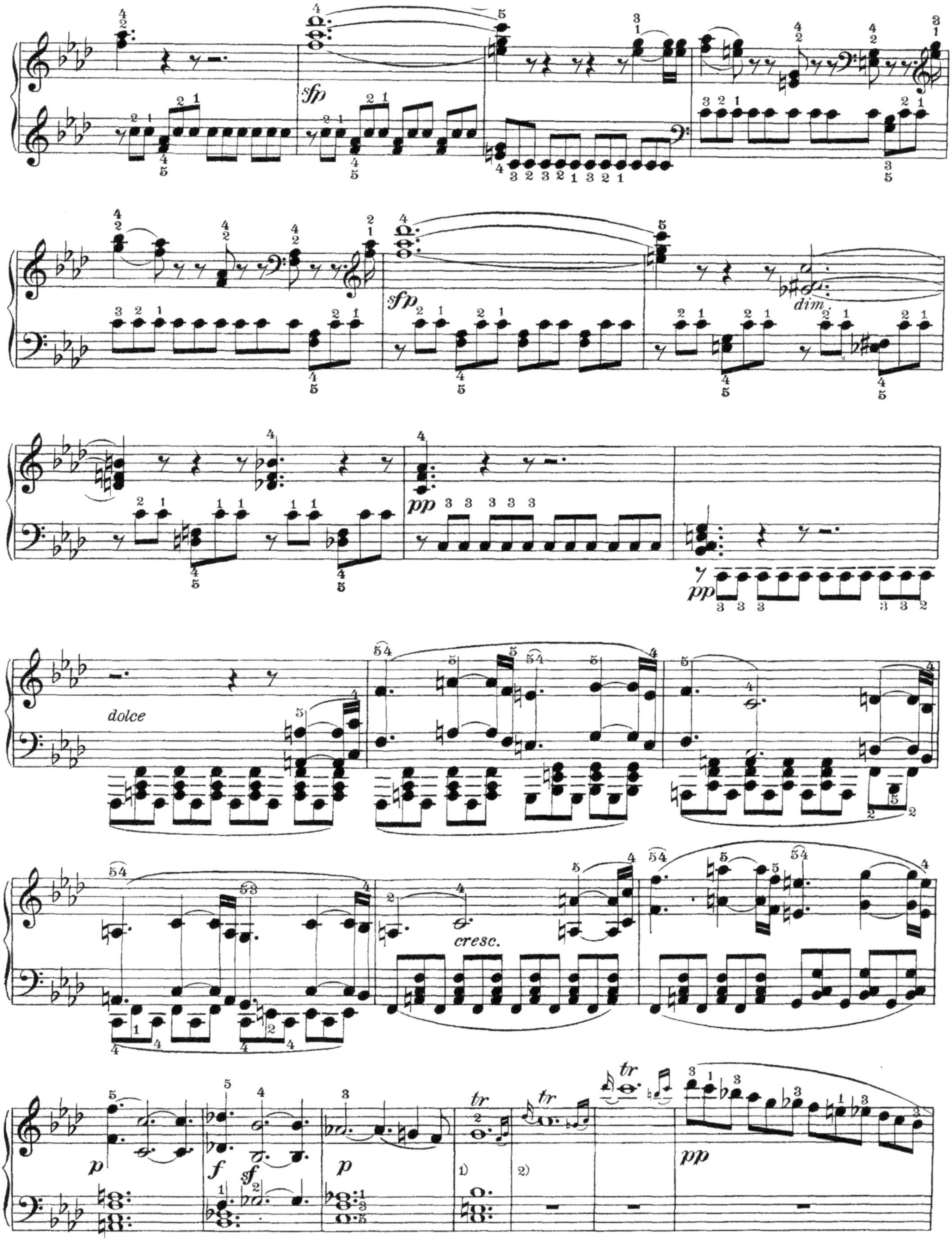
sfp
sfp
dim.
pp
pp
dolce
cresc.
p
f
sf
p
tr
1)
2)
tr
tr
pp

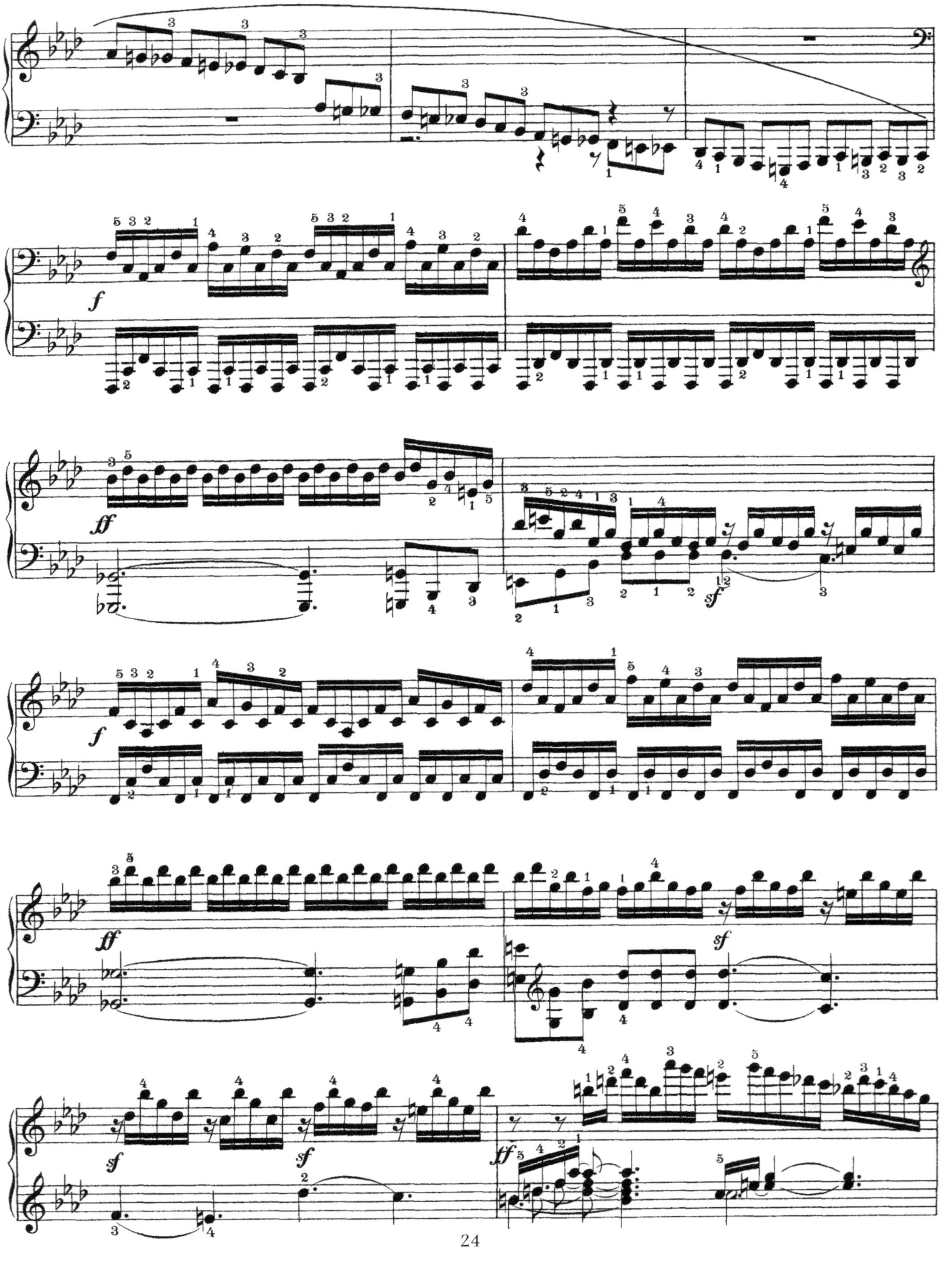

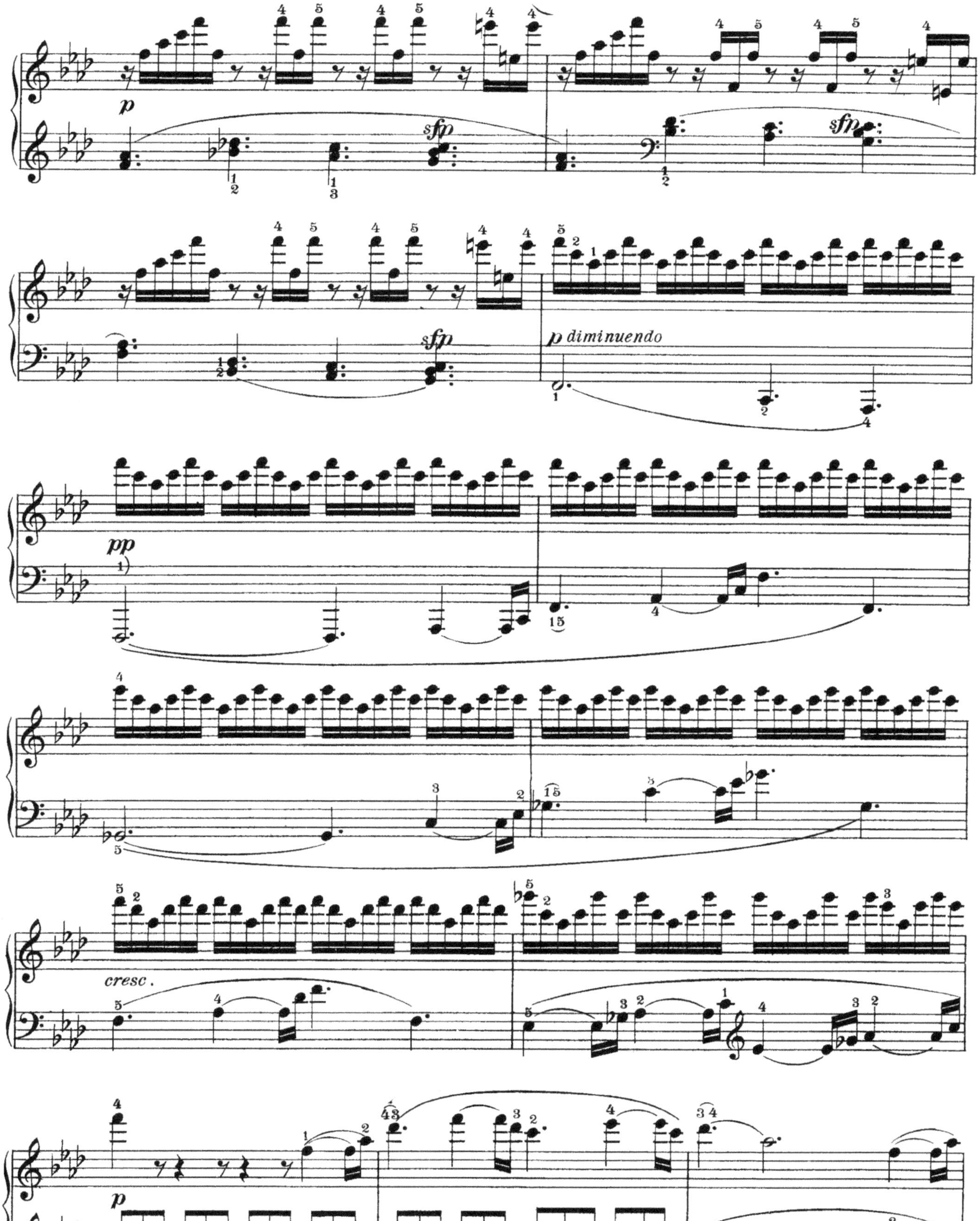

p
sfp
sfp
sfp
p diminuendo
pp
cresc.
p

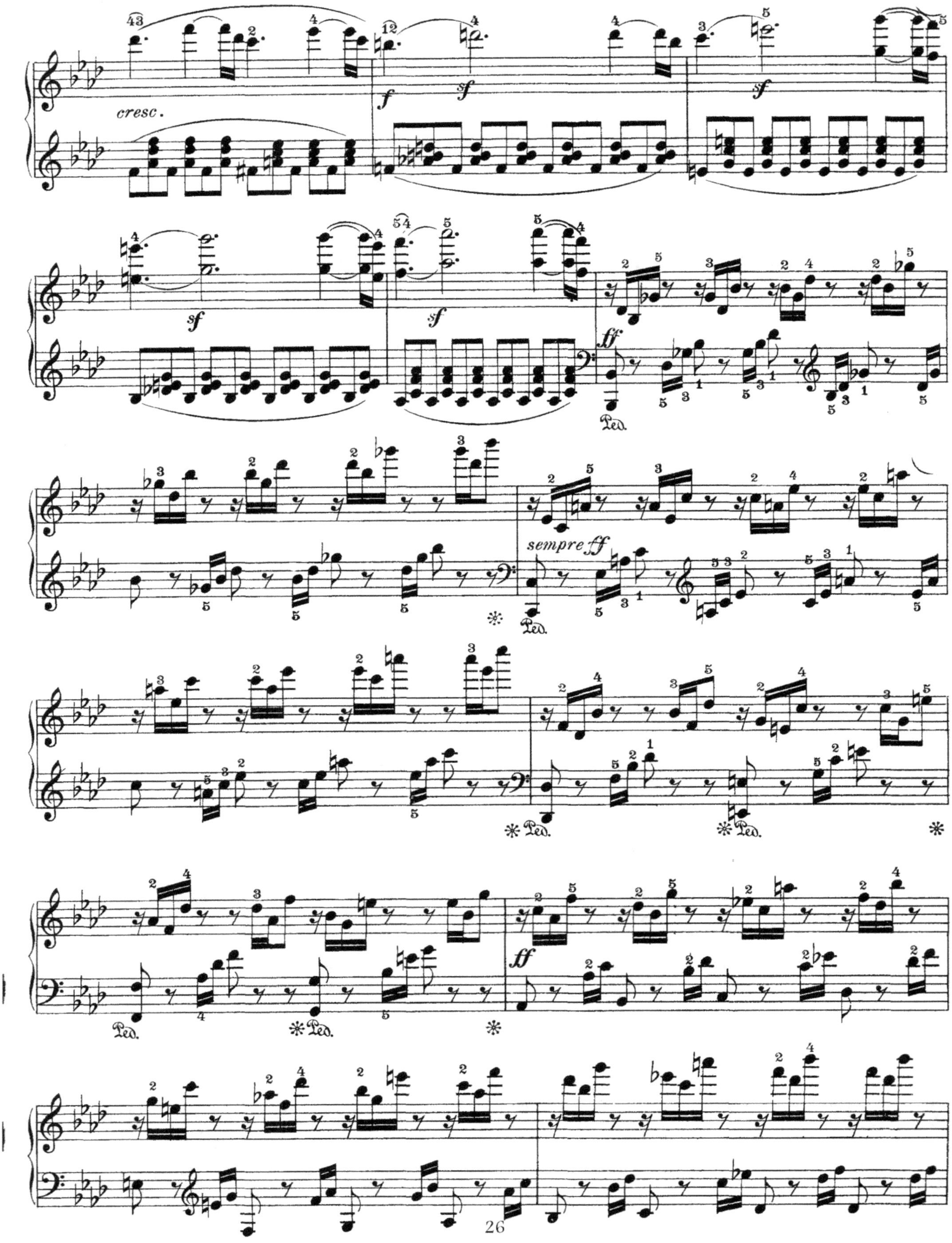
cresc.
f
sf
sf
sf
sf
ff
Ped.
sempre ff
Ped.
Ped.
Ped.
Ped.
Ped.
ff

ff
1)
(2 4 l. H.)
(2 4)
(4 2)
(2 4 2)
Ped.
230
(2 3 5 3 2)
sempre Ped.
p dimi - nu - en - do
ritar - dan - do
adagio.
pp p
sempre Ped.
più allegro.
cresc.
sf

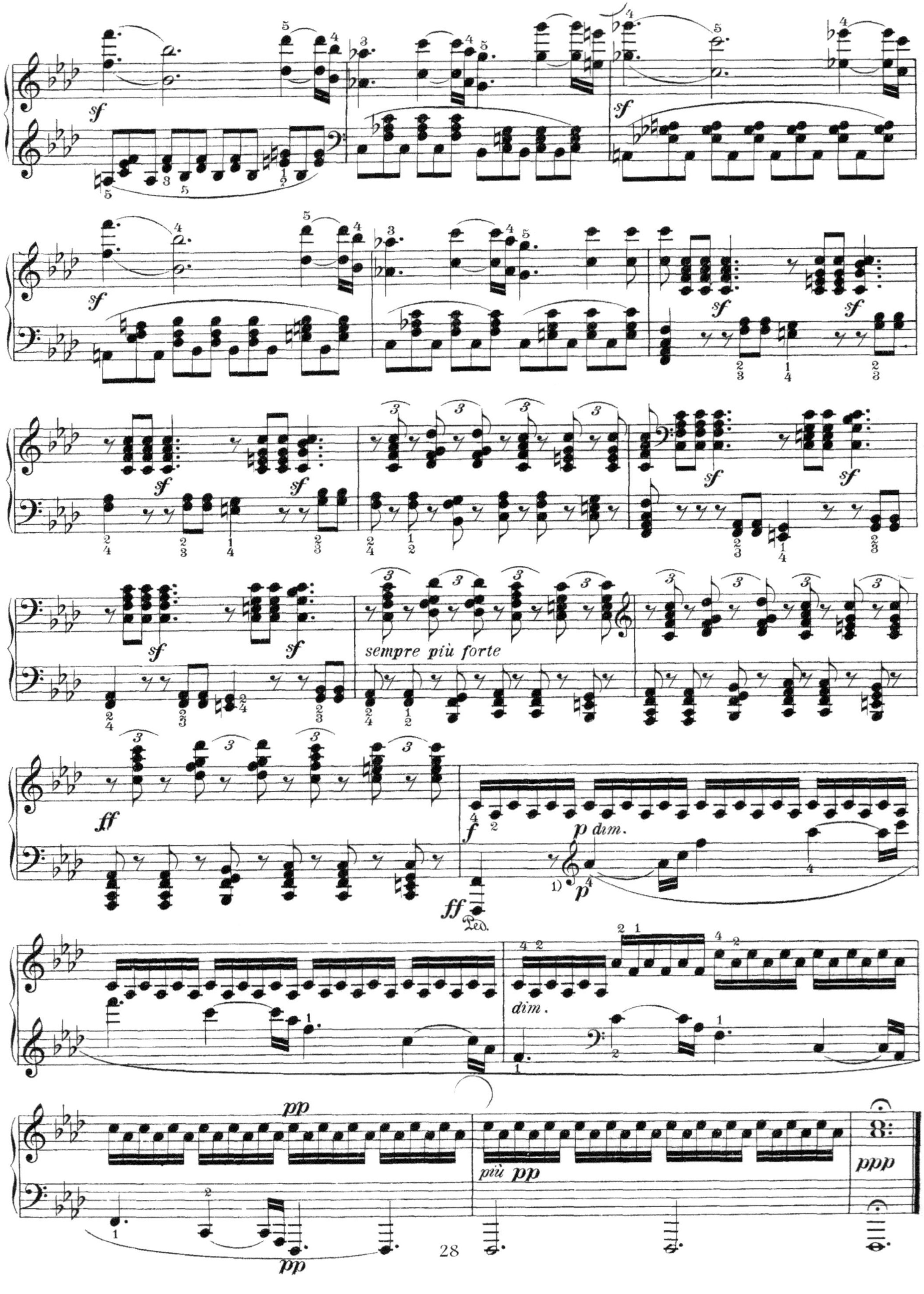
sf
sempre più forte
ff
f
p dim.
p
1)
Ped.
dim.
pp
più pp
ppp

Andante con moto.

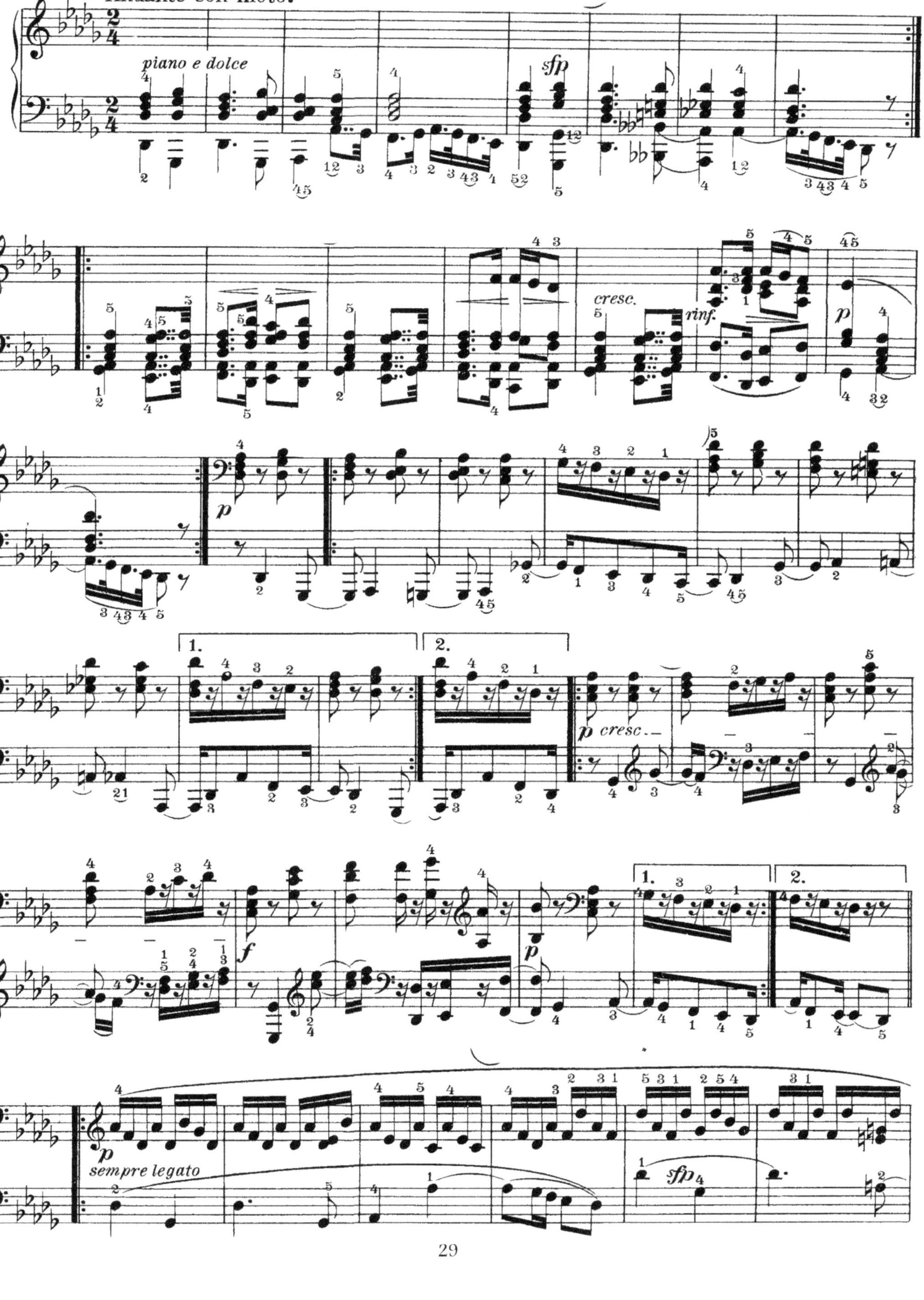

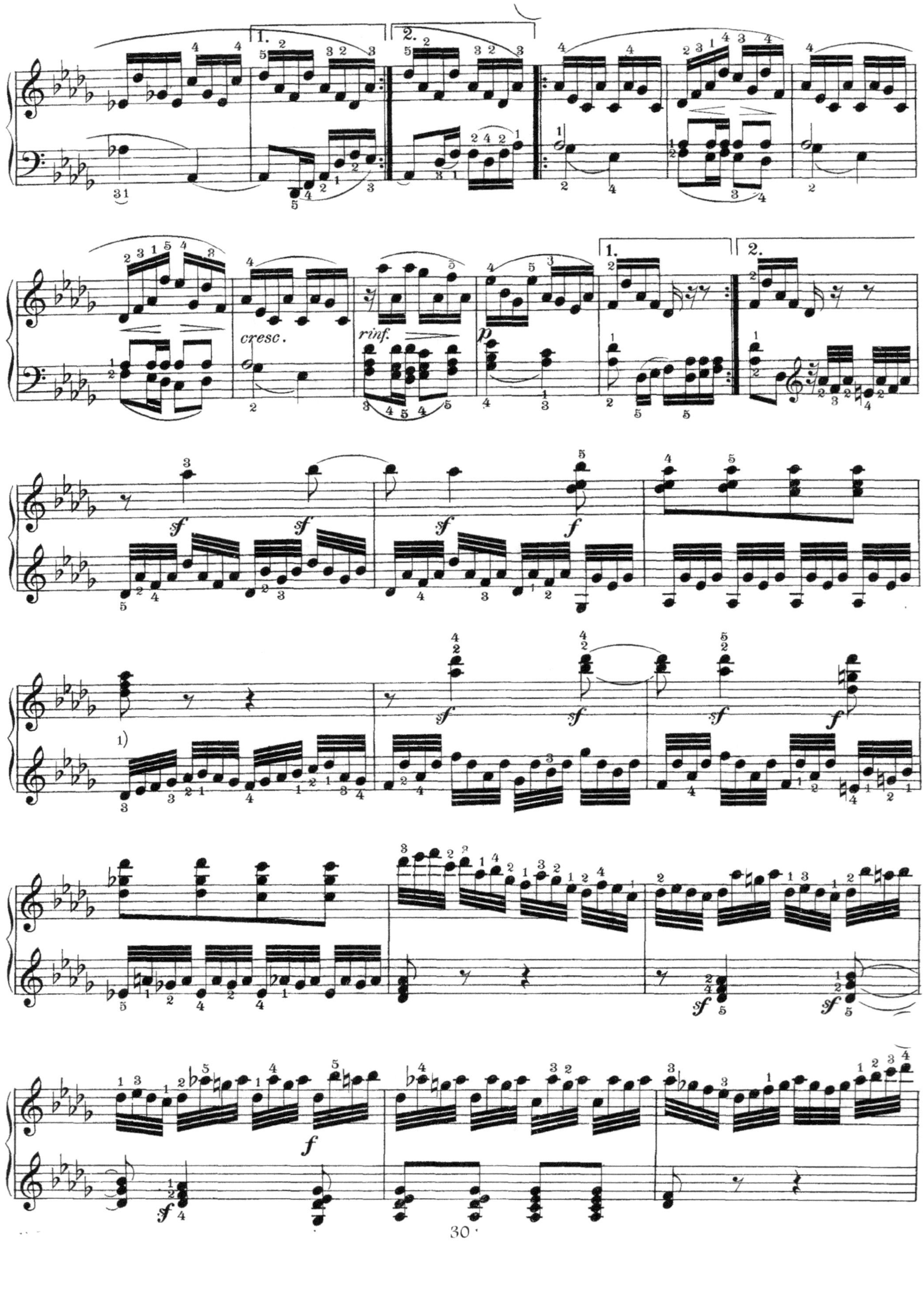
1.
2.
cresc.
rinf.
p
sf
f
1)

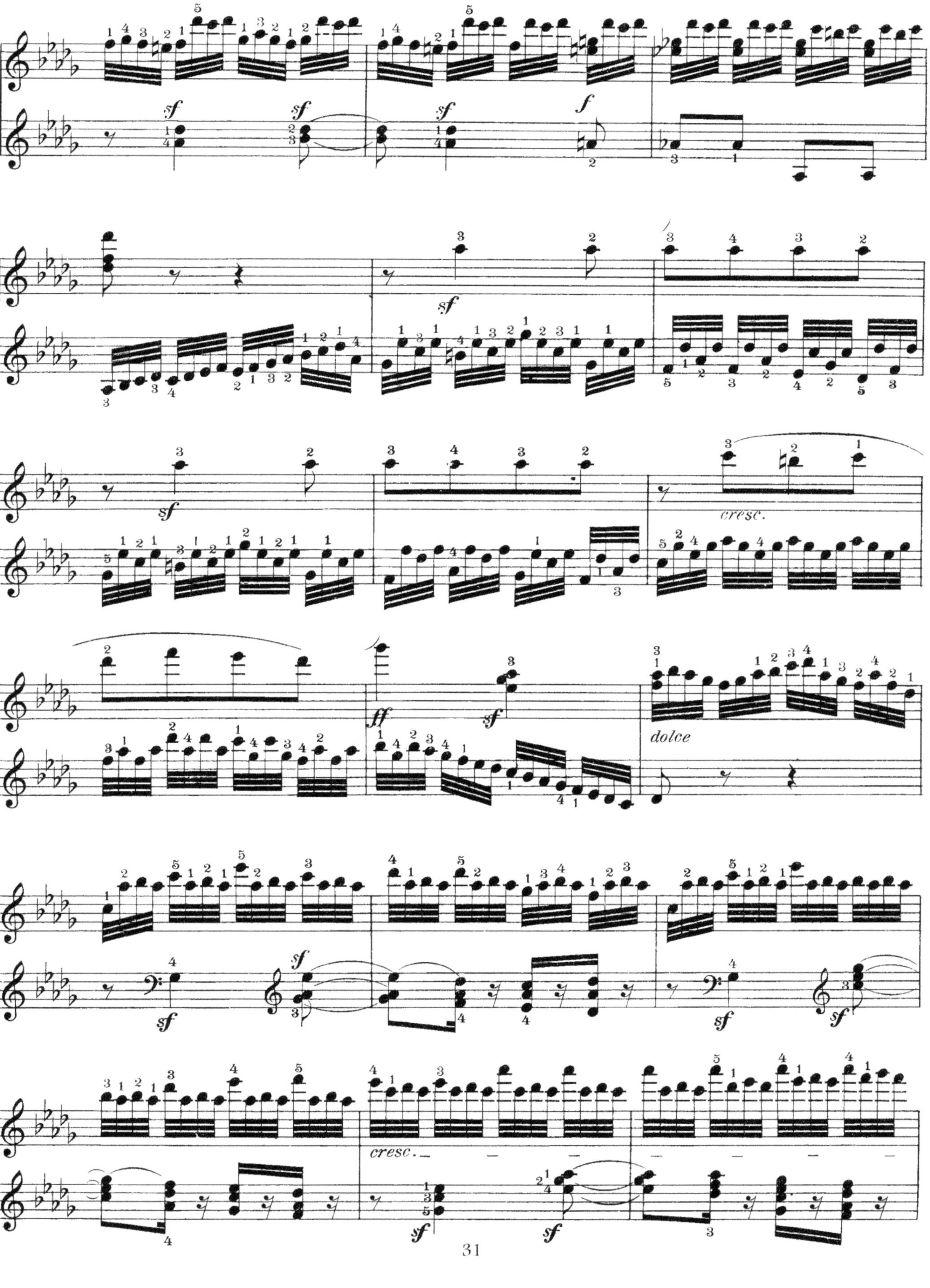
sf
sf
sf
f
sf
sf
cresc.
ff
sf
dolce
sf
sf
sf
sf
cresc.
sf
sf

Allegro ma non troppo.

32

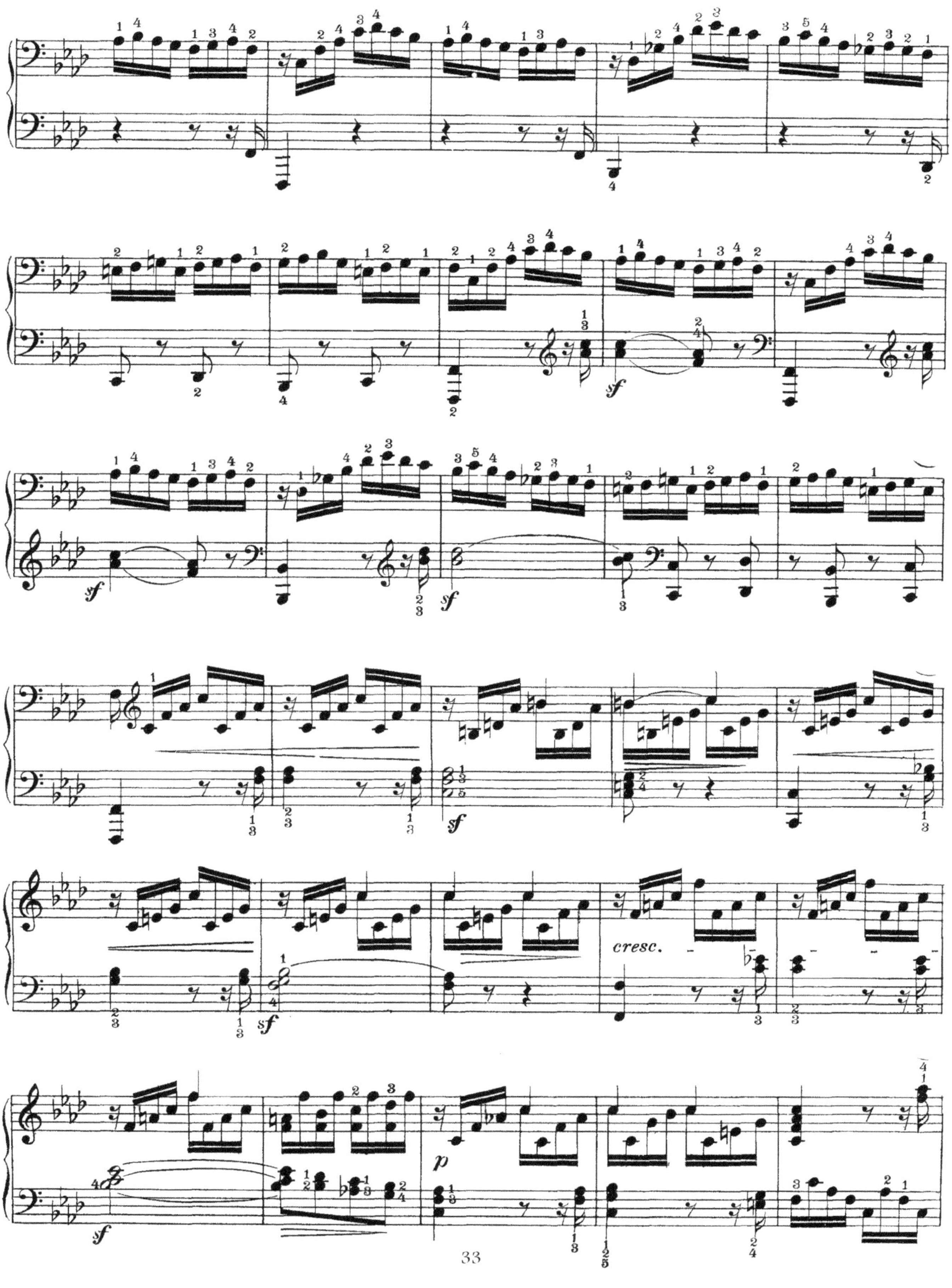
cresc.

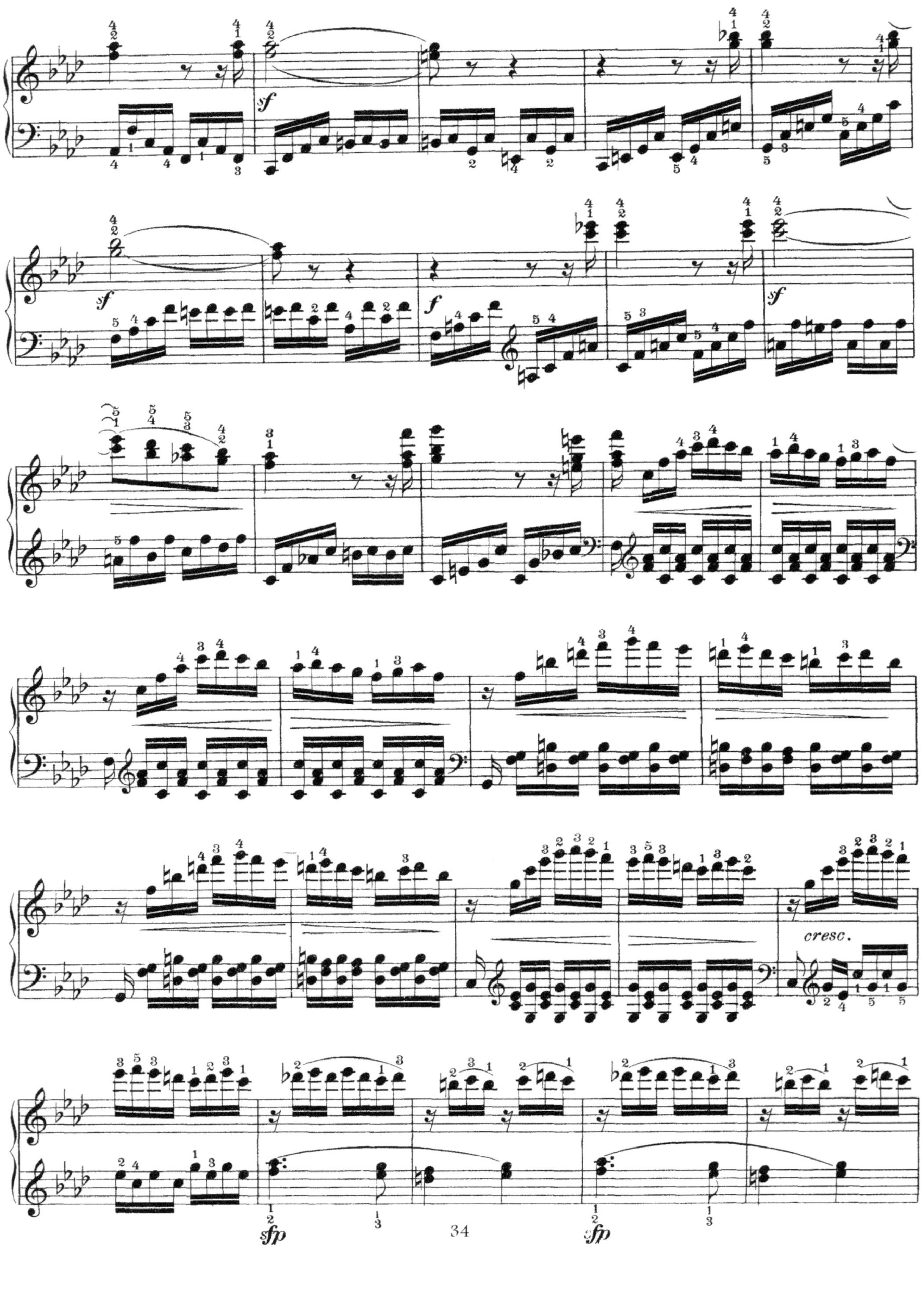
sf
sf
f
sf
cresc.
sfp
sfp

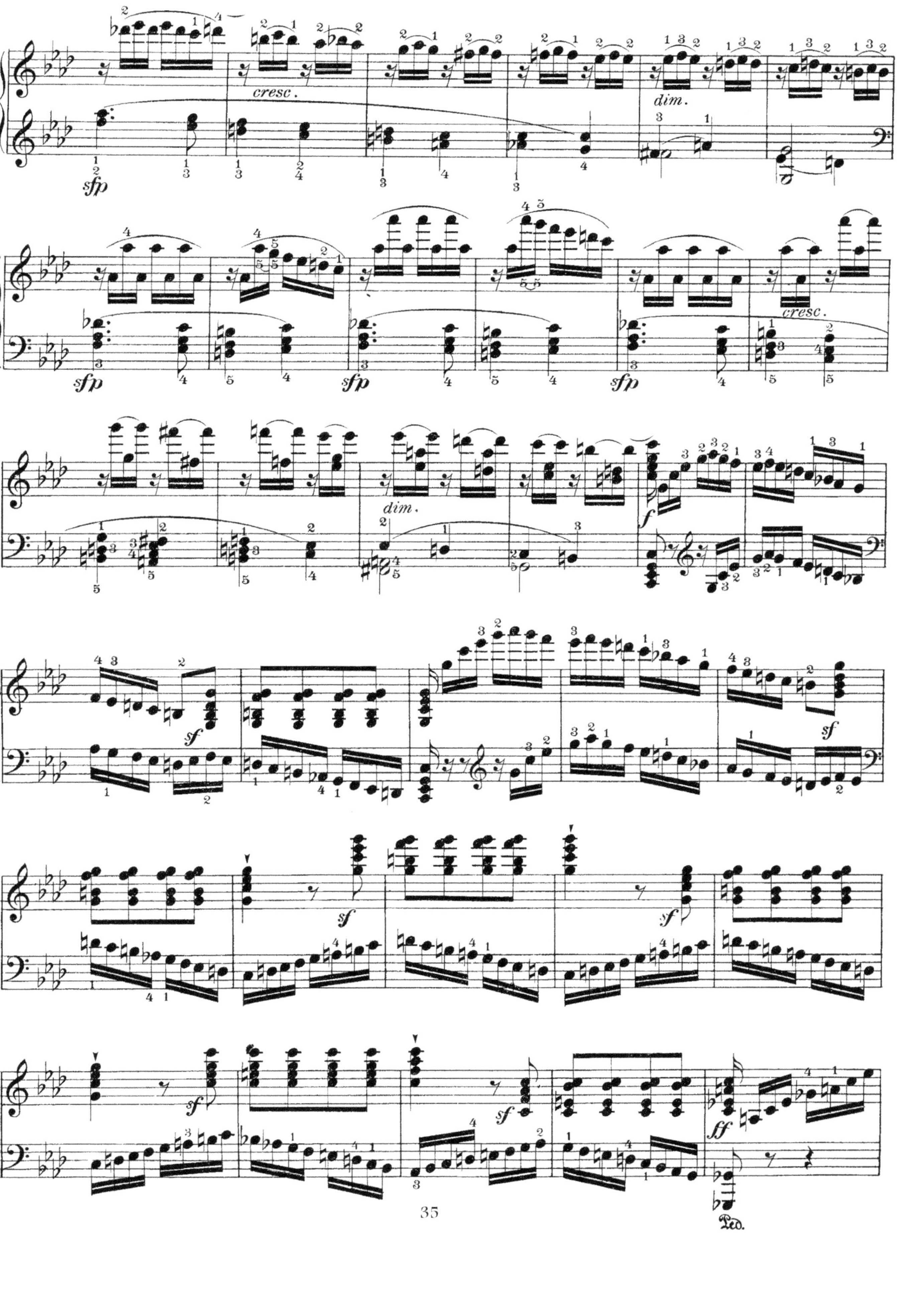
cresc.
sfp
dim.
sfp
sfp
sfp
cresc.
dim.
f
sf
sf
sf
sf
sf
ff
Ped.

la seconda parte due volte

36

sfp
sfp
sf
sempre forte
sf
sf
sfp
sfp
sfp
sf
sempre forte
sf
sf
più f
ff
[p]
[cresc.]
8

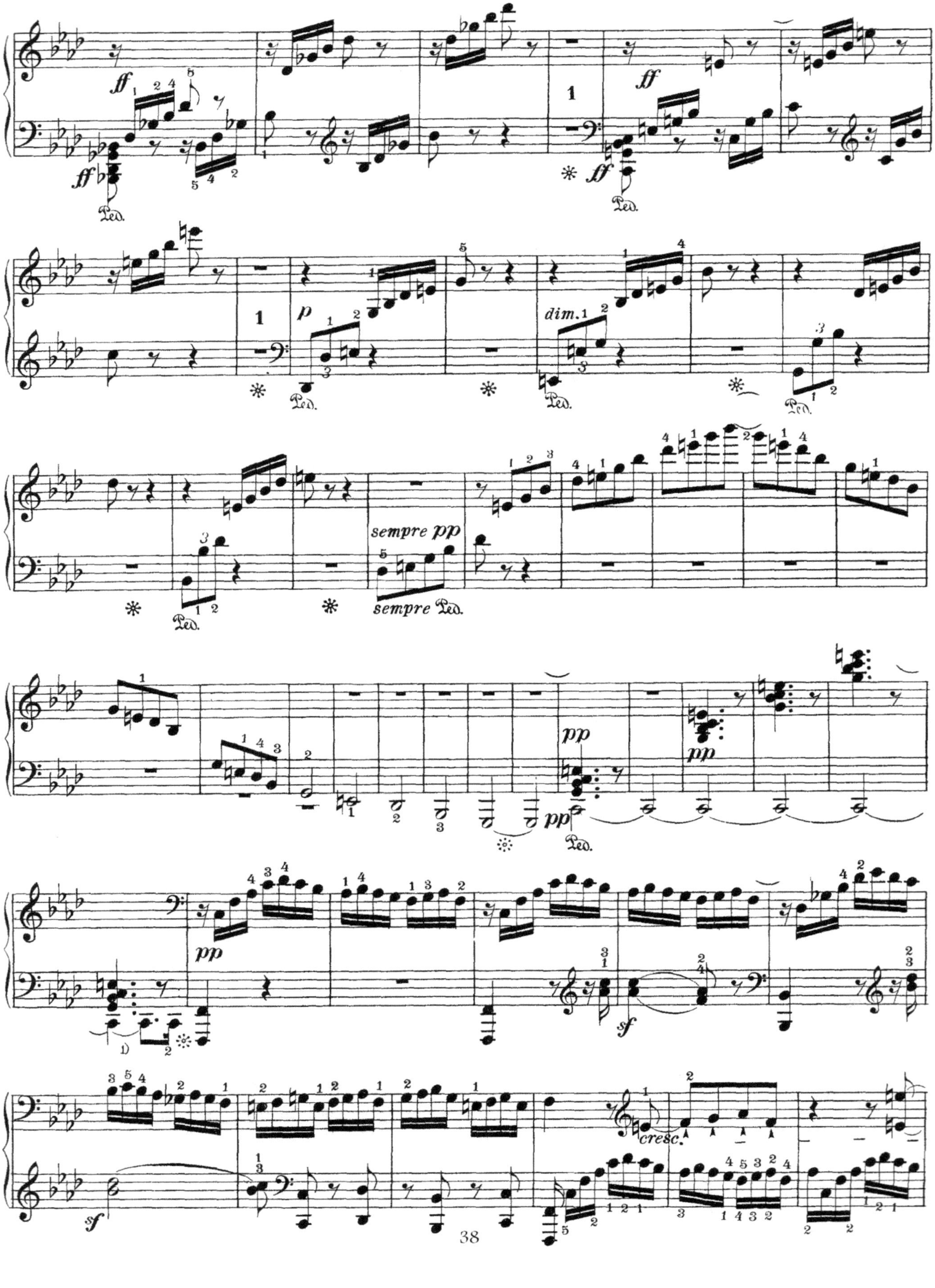
ff
Ped.
p
dim.
sempre pp
sempre Ped.
pp
cresc.
sf

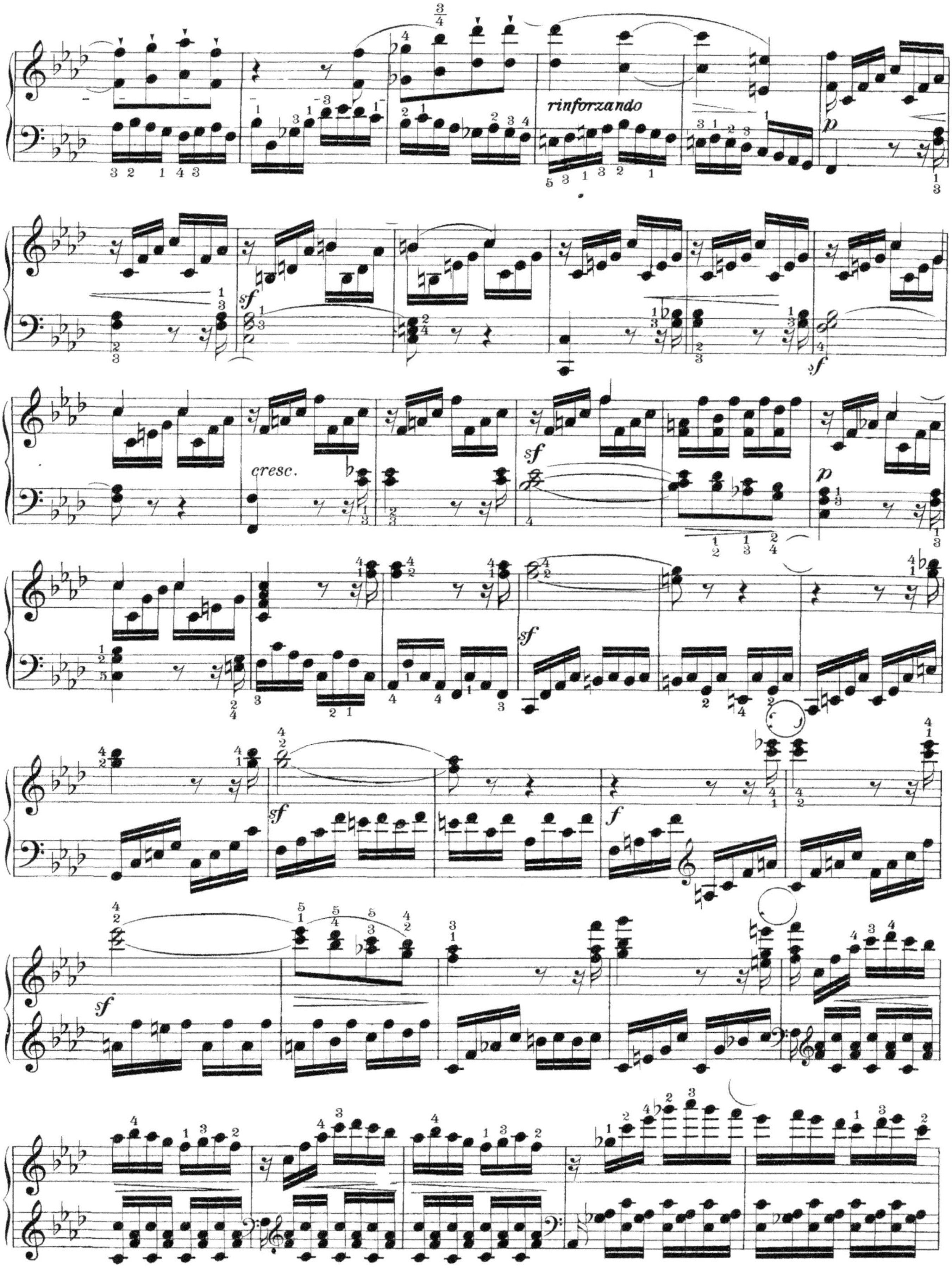
rinforzando
cresc.

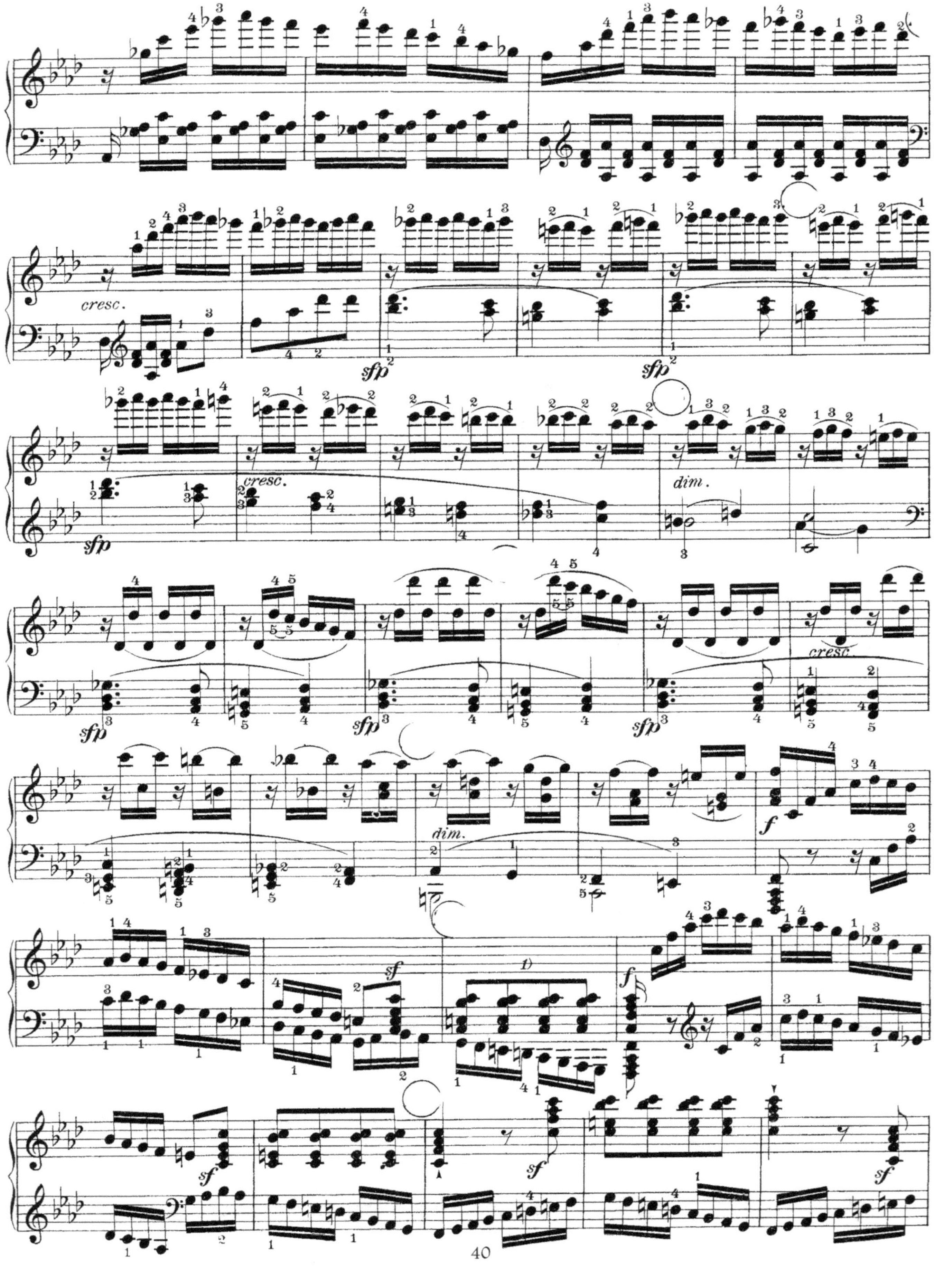
cresc.
sfp
sfp
sfp
cresc.
dim.
sfp
sfp
sfp
cresc.
dim.
f
sf
f
sf
sf
sf

cresc.
ff
Ped.
dim.
sf
sempre più allegro
più forte
presto.
ff
sf
p
f

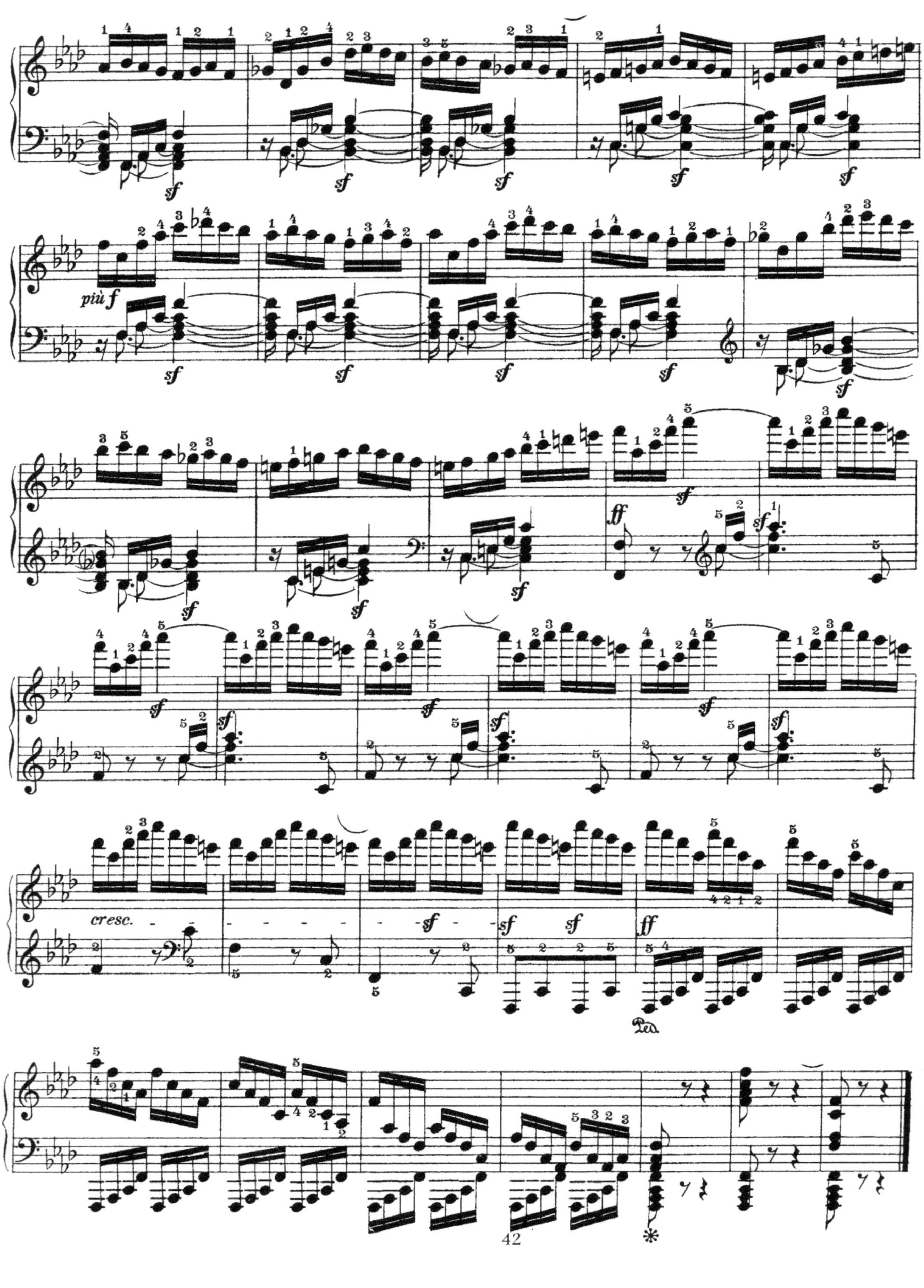
più f
cresc.
Ped.

Prelude
in C# minor

Sergei Rachmaninoff
Op.3, No.2

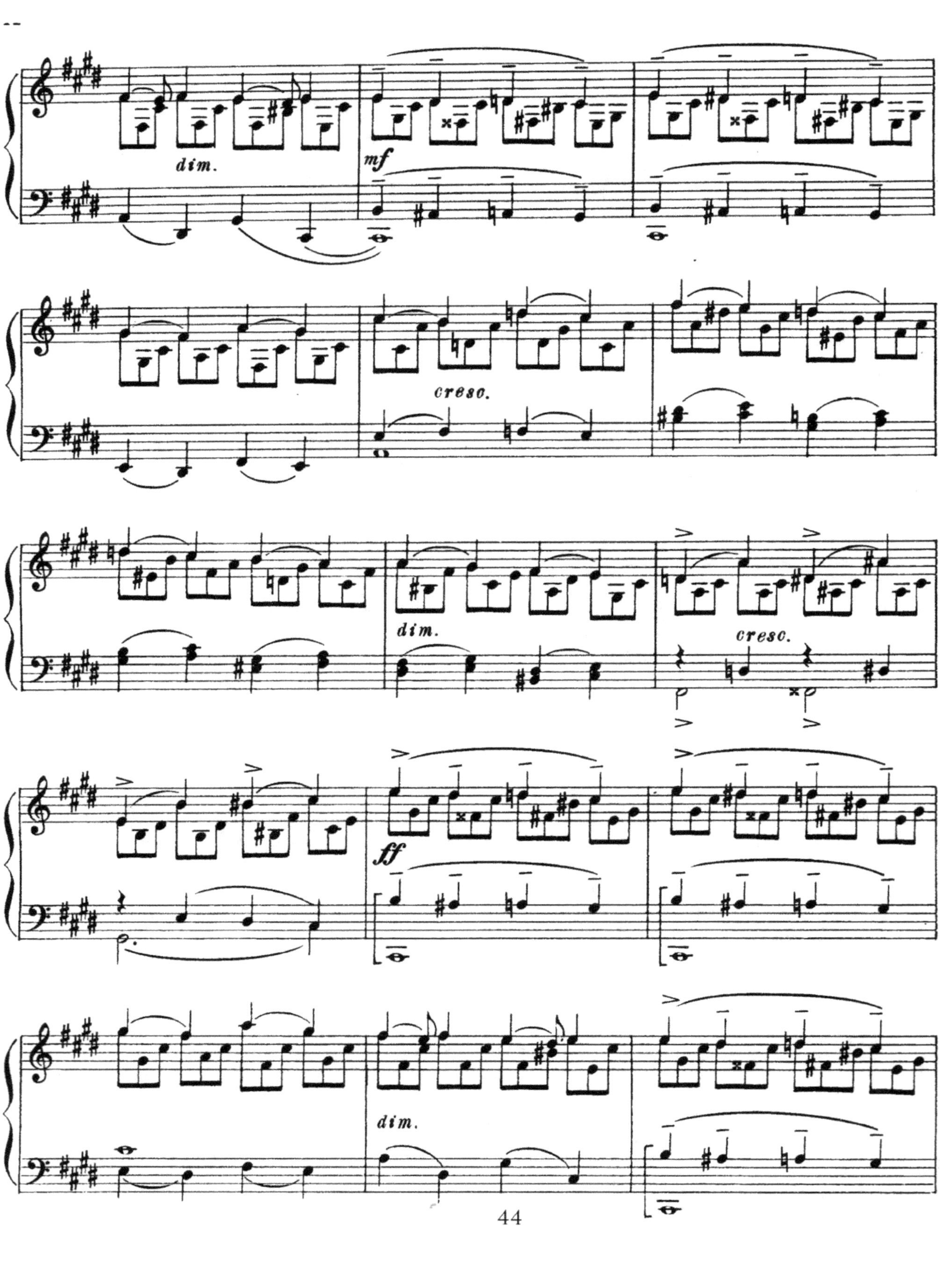
dim.
mf
cresc.
dim.
cresc.
ff
dim.

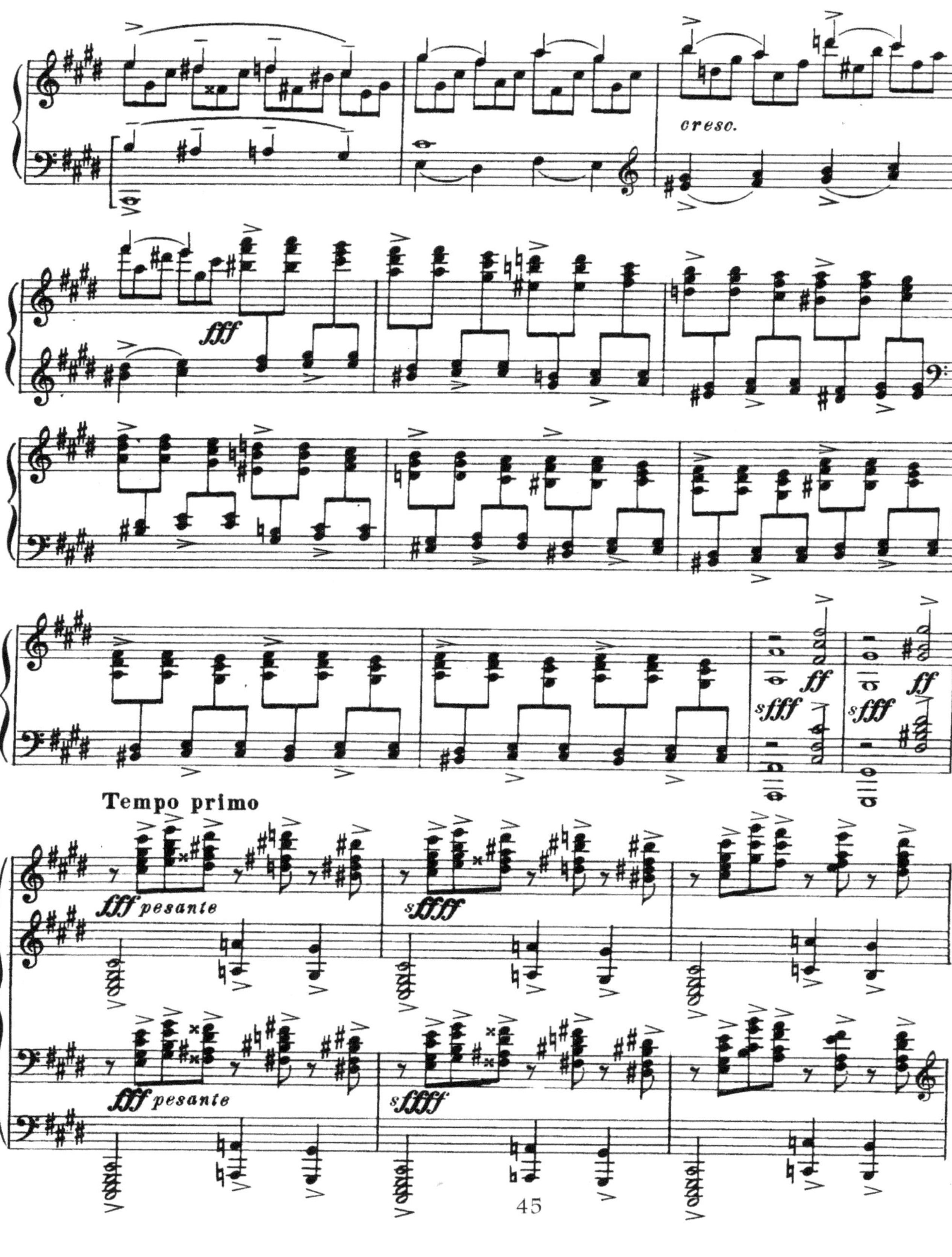
cresc.
fff
sfff
ff
Tempo primo
fff pesante
sffff

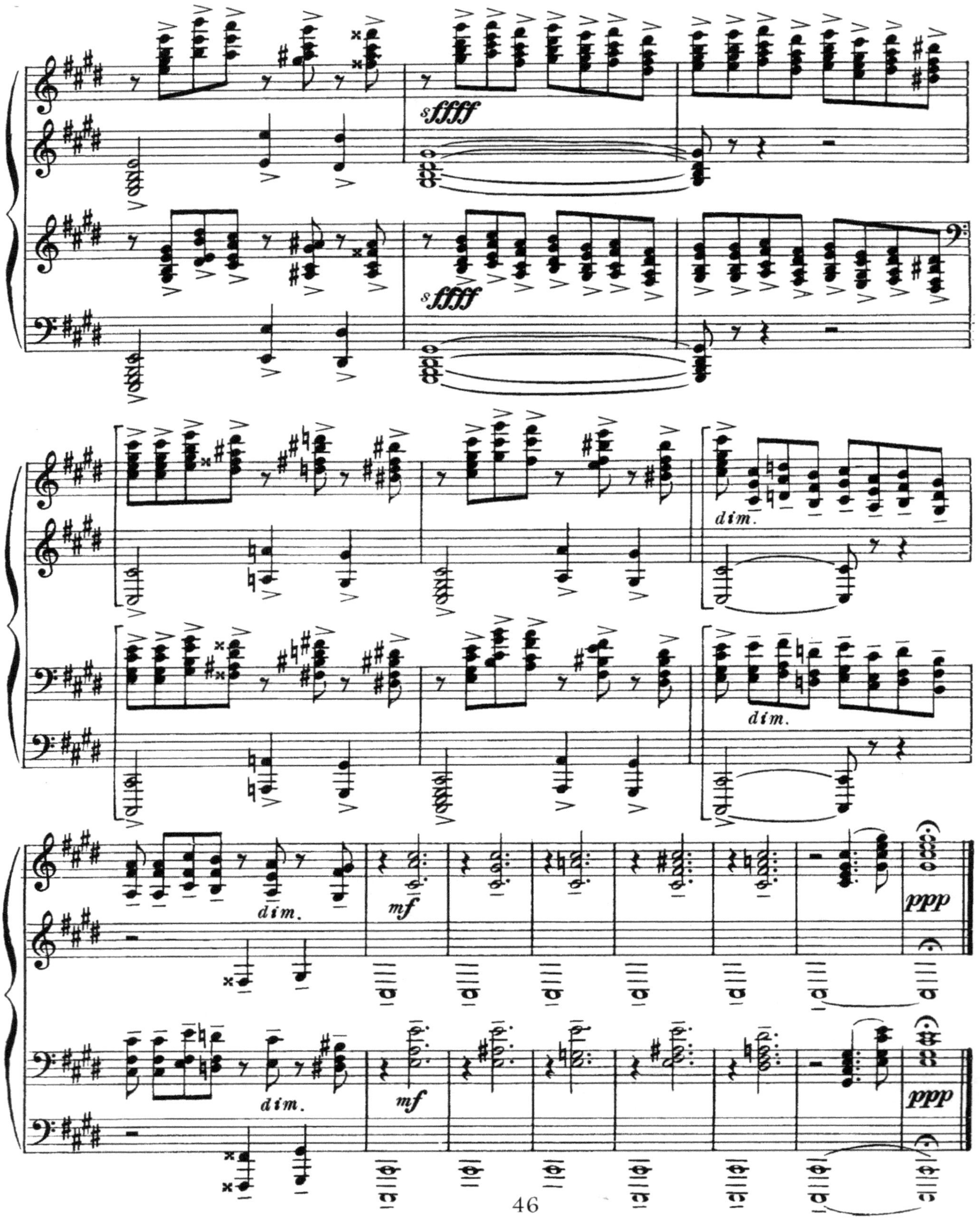
sffff
sffff
dim.
dim.
dim.
mf
ppp
dim.
mf
ppp

Sonata, Part 7
Apres une Lecture du Dante

Franz Liszt

47

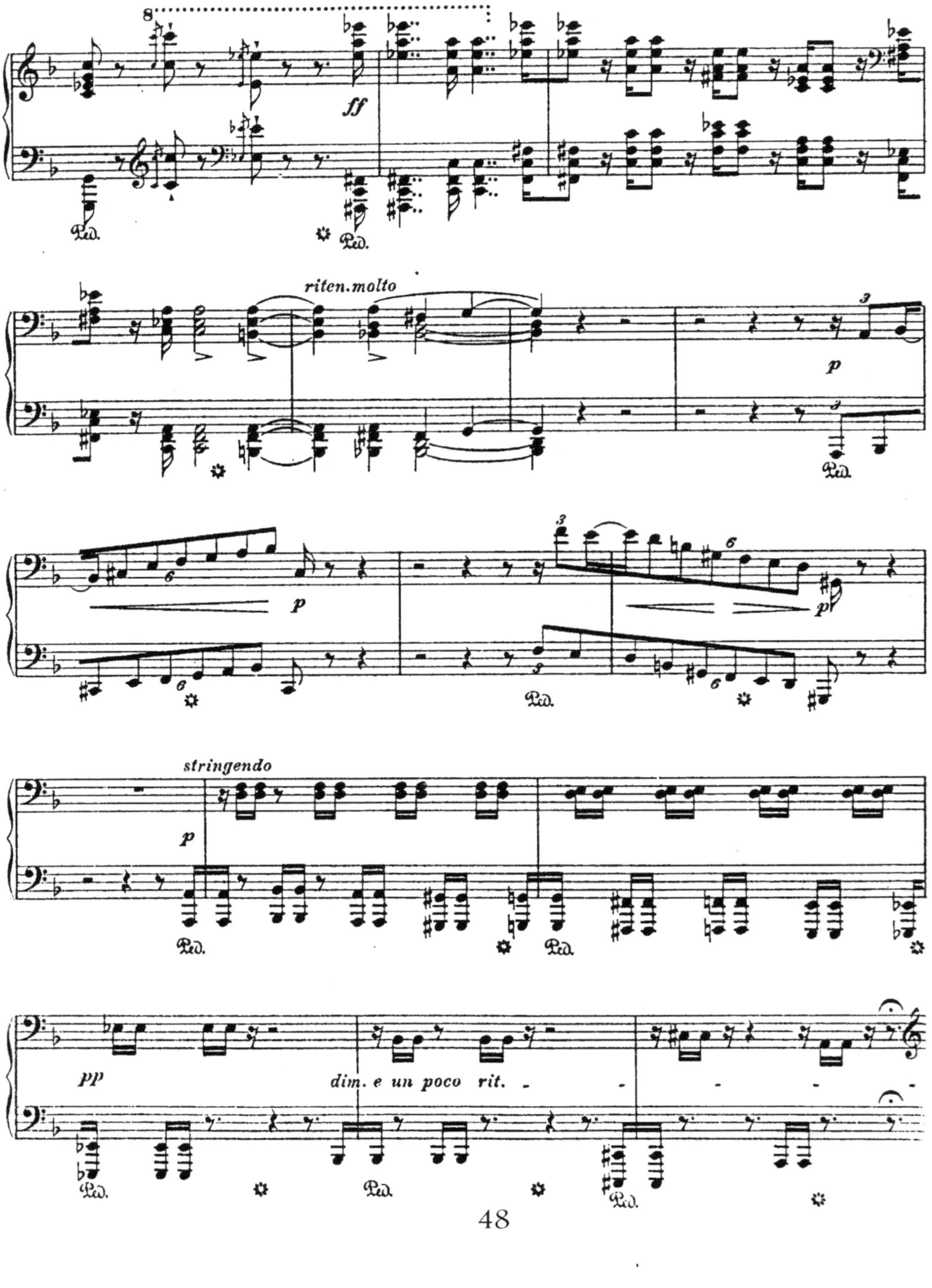

8
ff
Ped.
riten. molto
p
stringendo
pp
dim. e un poco rit.

Presto agitato assai.
p lamentoso
Ped.
sempre legato
diminuendo
Ped.

più crescendo
rfz
ff con impeto
marcatissimo
mf disperato
Ped.

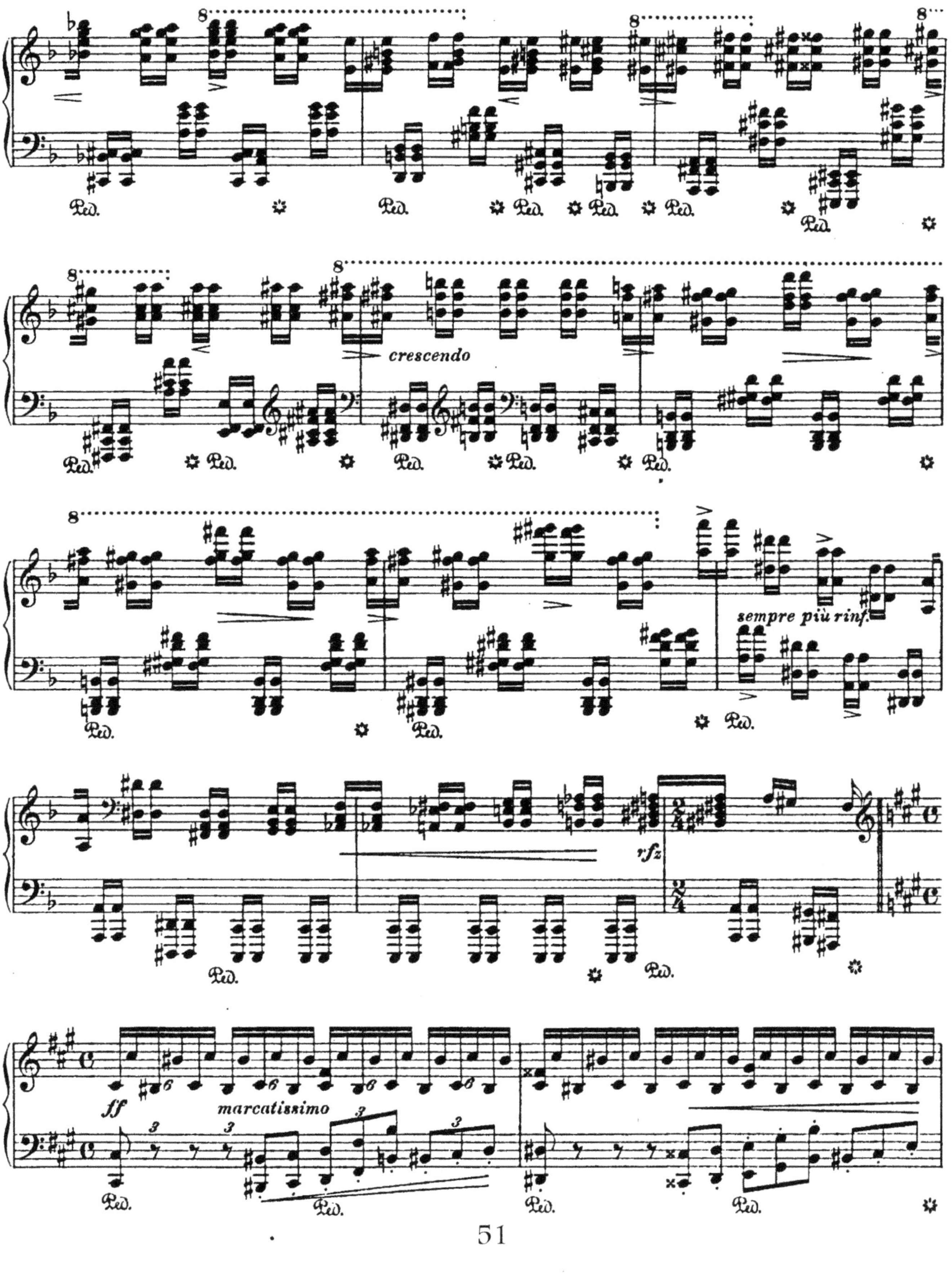
crescendo
sempre più rinf.
rfz
ff
marcatissimo
Ped.

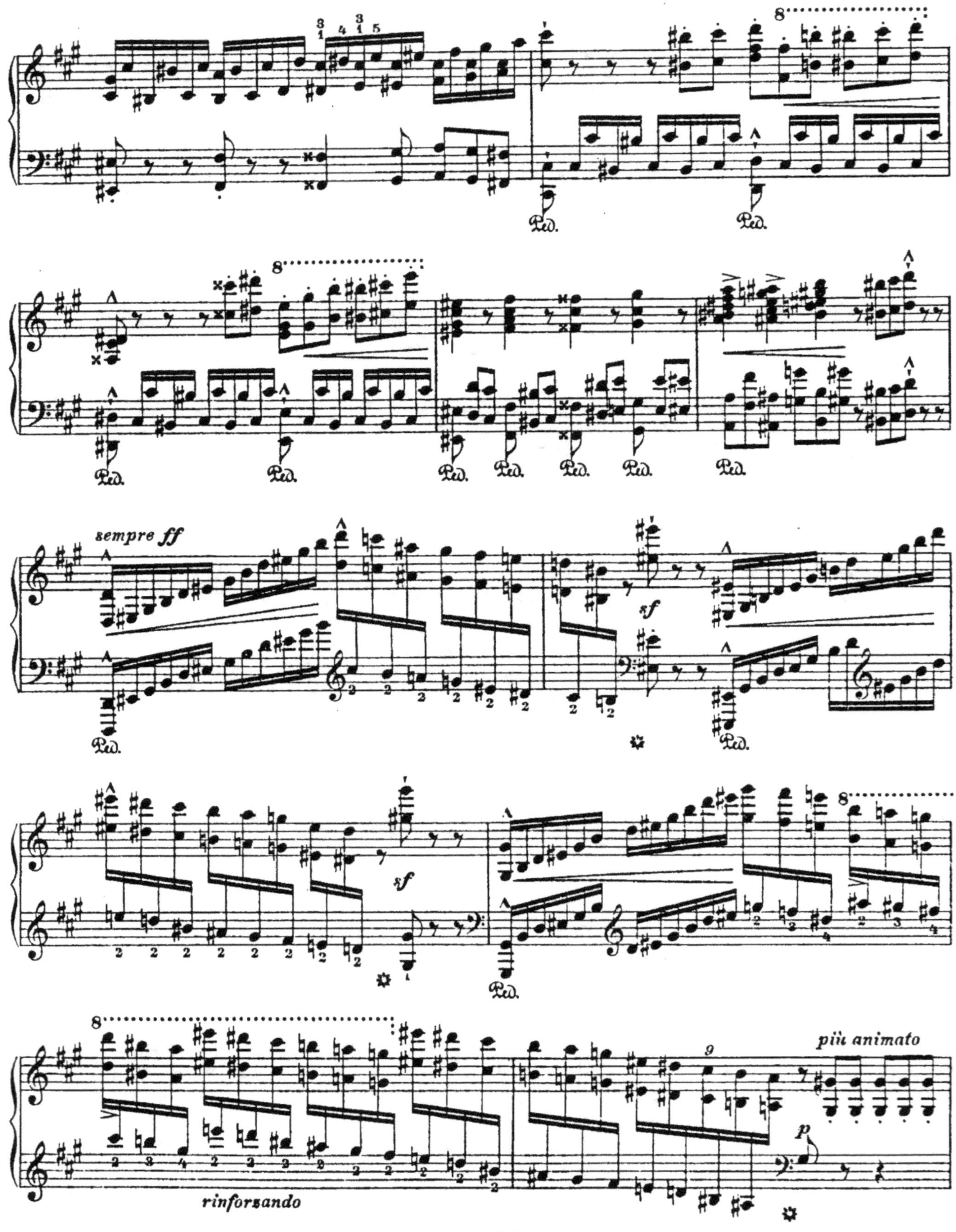
Ped.
sempre ff
sf
rinforzando
più animato
p

sempre staccato
crescendo
8
Ped.
crescendo molto
rinforzando
fff
precipitato
sf

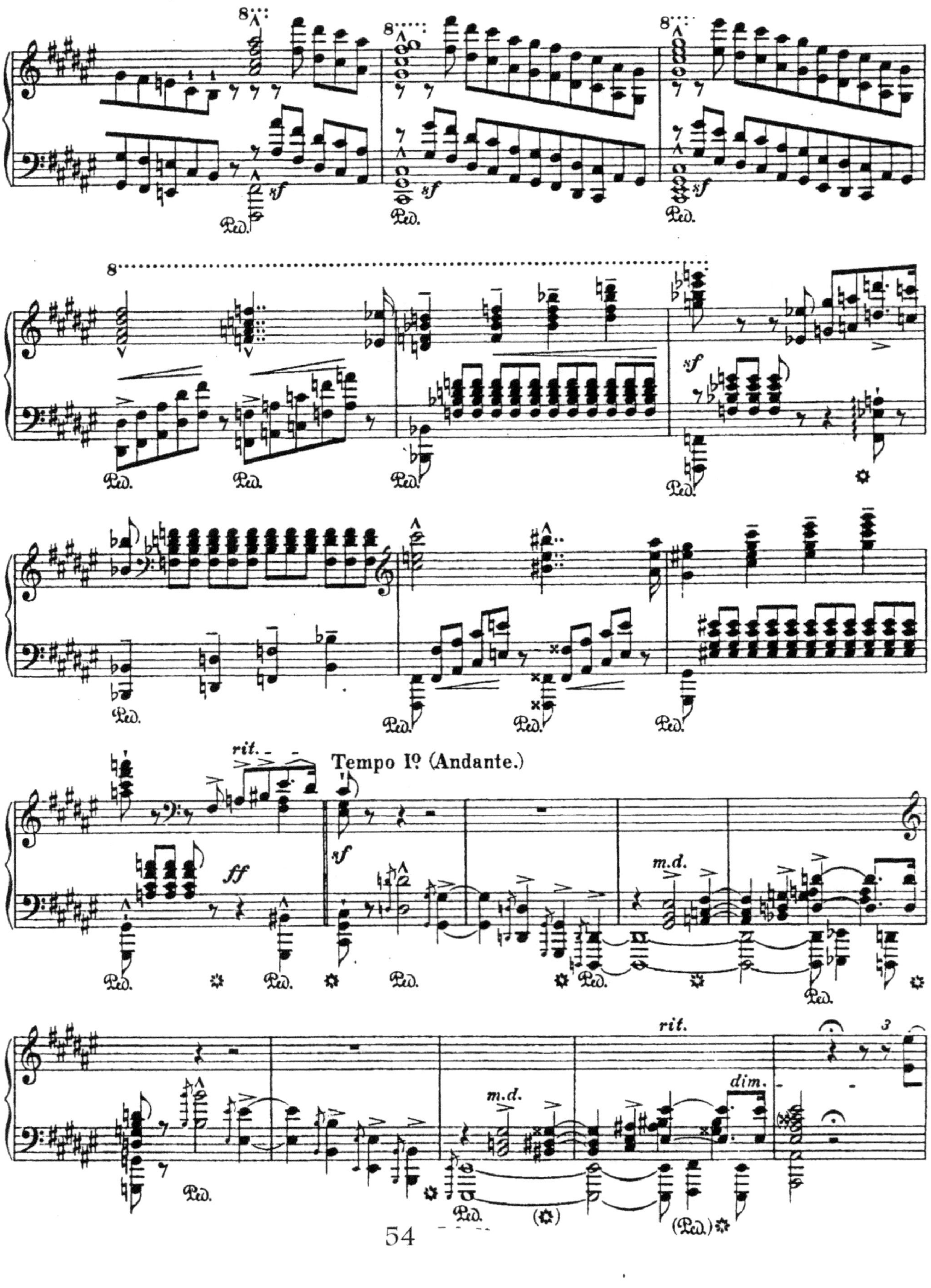
sf
Ped.
rit.
Tempo Iº (Andante.)
ff
m.d.
dim.
(Ped.)

Andante quasi improvisato.
dolcissimo con intimo sentimento
una corda
Ped.
ppp
espressivo
dolce
molto rit.
lunga Pausa
pp
Andante.
ben marcato il canto
sempre legato

rit.
un poco rallentando
p
lagrimoso
poco rinforz.
Recitativo.
Adagio.
Ped.

più tosto ritenuto e rubato quasi improvvisato
ppp dolcissimo con amore
2 Ped.
affrettando
più crescendo ed appassionato
rall.
poco rallentando

58

Con 8va ad libitum
ff appassionato assai
Allegro moderato.
pp sotto voce
sempre p
pp tremolando
un poco
marcato
mf

sempre p
Ped.
p
p agitato
Ped.
poco a poco crescendo
Ped.
Ped.
Ped.
8
più crescendo
Ped.
Ped.
8
8
Ped.

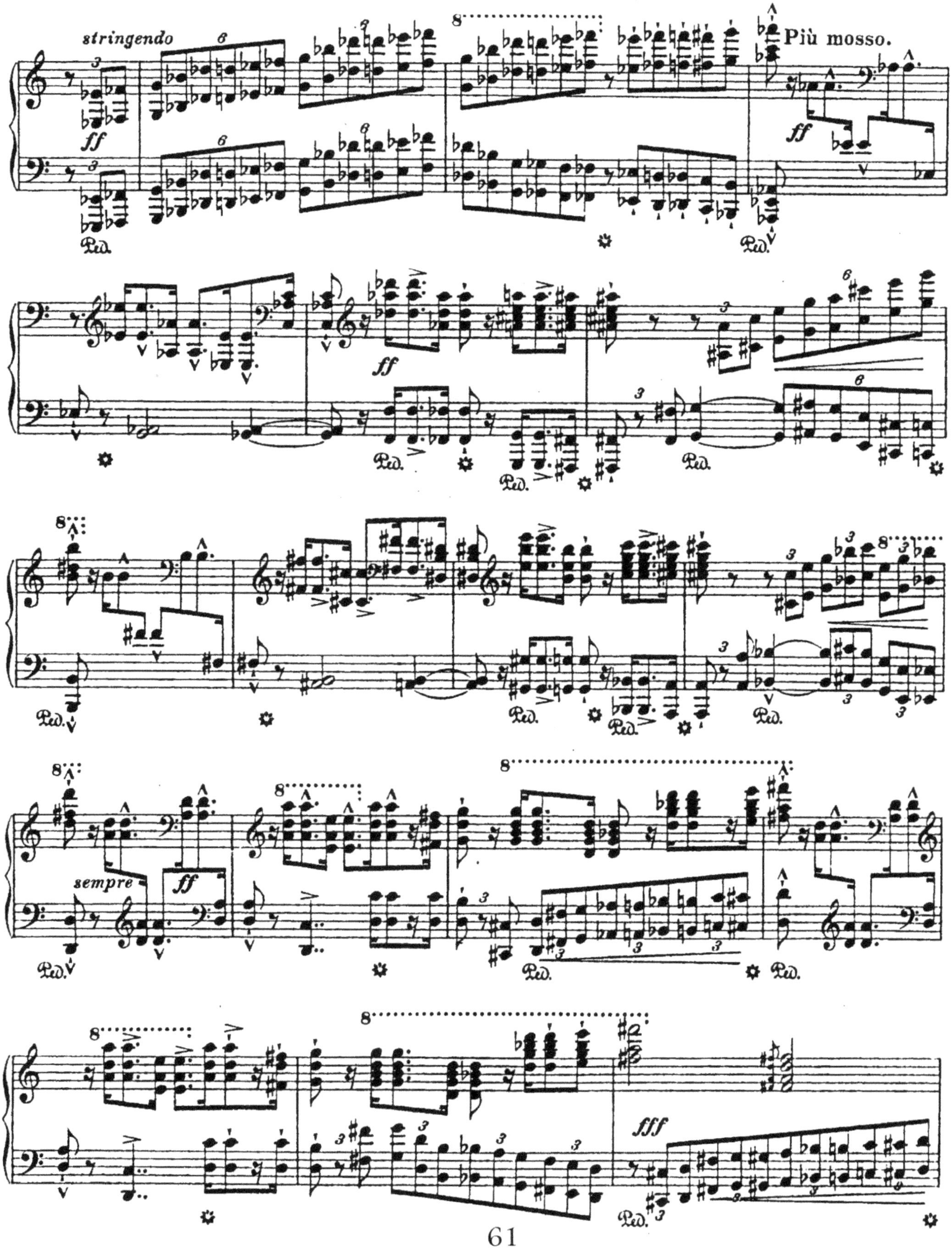
stringendo
ff
Più mosso.
ff
ff
ff
sempre
ff
fff
Ped.

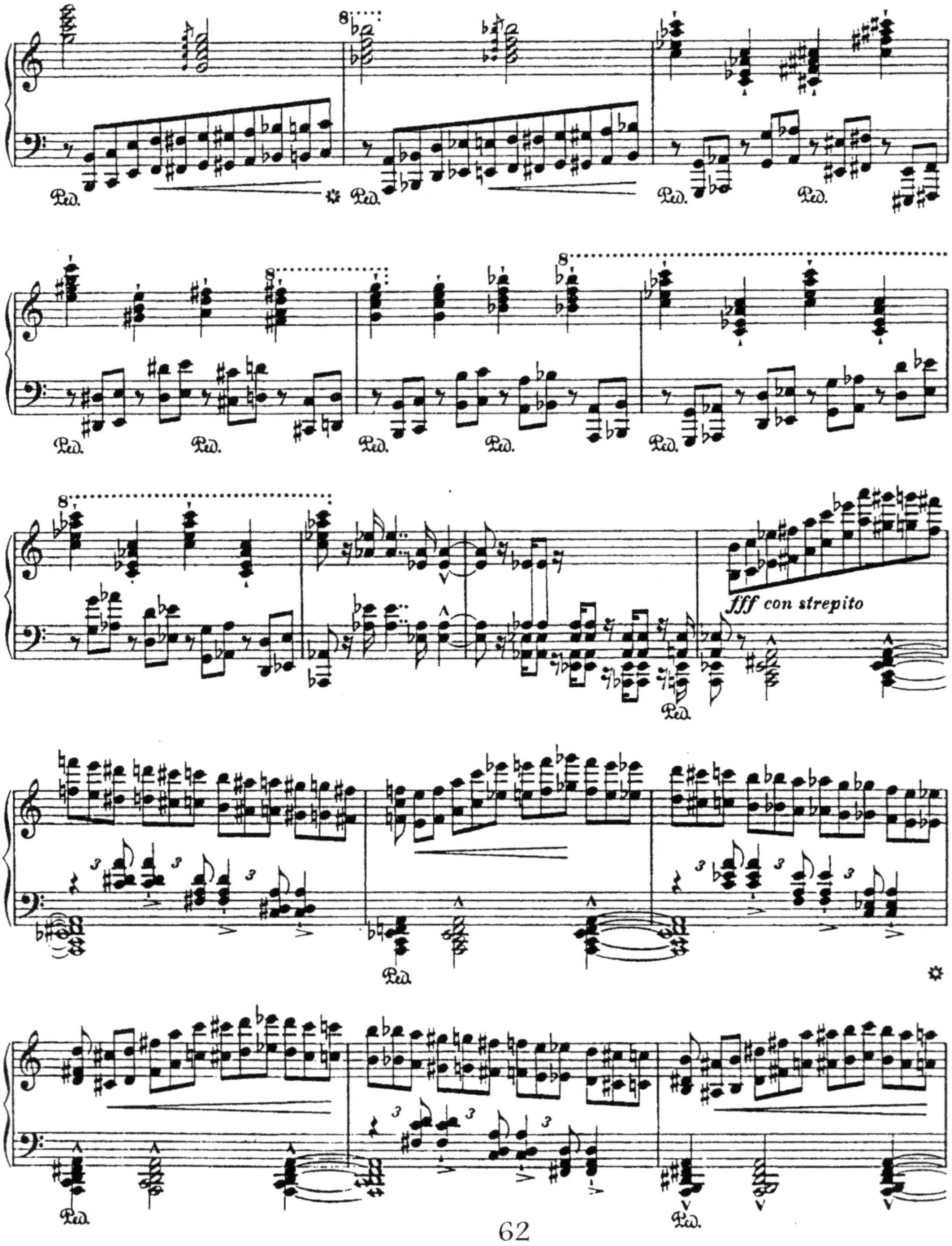
fff con strepito

sempre marcatissimo
diminuendo poco a poco
senza rallentare
più diminuendo

64

Andante.
pp tremolando
marcato poco riten.
crescendo
Più mosso.
sf
stringendo
ff
Allegro.
fff

poco a poco più di moto

Allegro vivace.
ff molto appassionato
sempre marcatissimo
sf
Presto.
p
cresc.

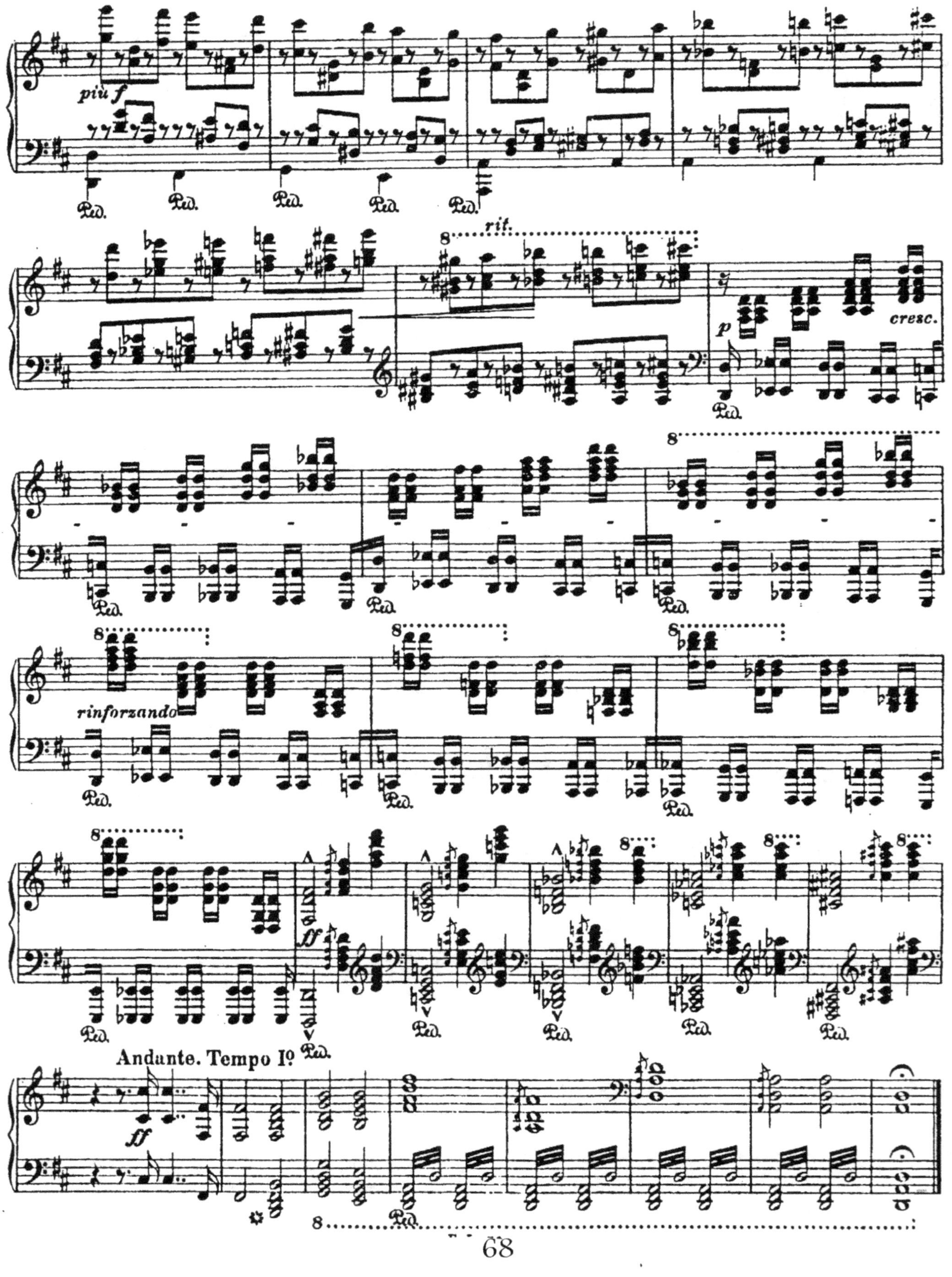
più f
Ped.
rit.
8
p
cresc.
rinforzando
ff
Andante. Tempo Iº
ff

Nocturne

Frederic Francois Chopin
Op. 72, No. 1

tenuto
p
poco a poco cresc.
f
sf
dim.
sempre dim.
pp (una corda)
aspiratamente
cresc.
poco f
Ped.

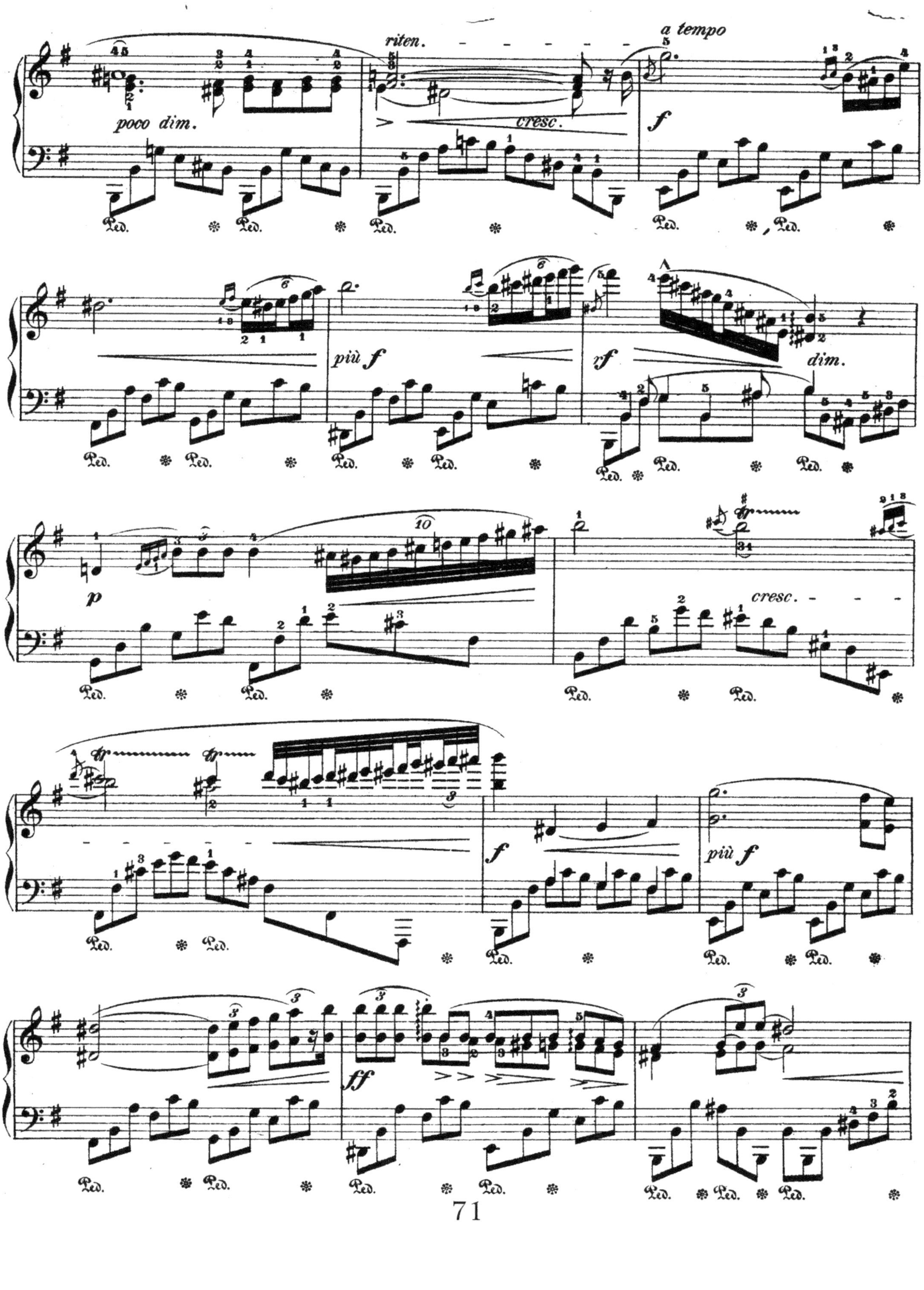
poco dim.
riten.
cresc.
a tempo
f
più f
rf
dim.
p
cresc.
f
più f
ff
Ped.

sf
dim.
dim.
p
pp dolcissimo
una corda
poco cresc.
dim.
dolce
psf
sempre più p
pp calando

Toccata
in D minor

Johan Sebastian Bach

Adagio

Prestissimo

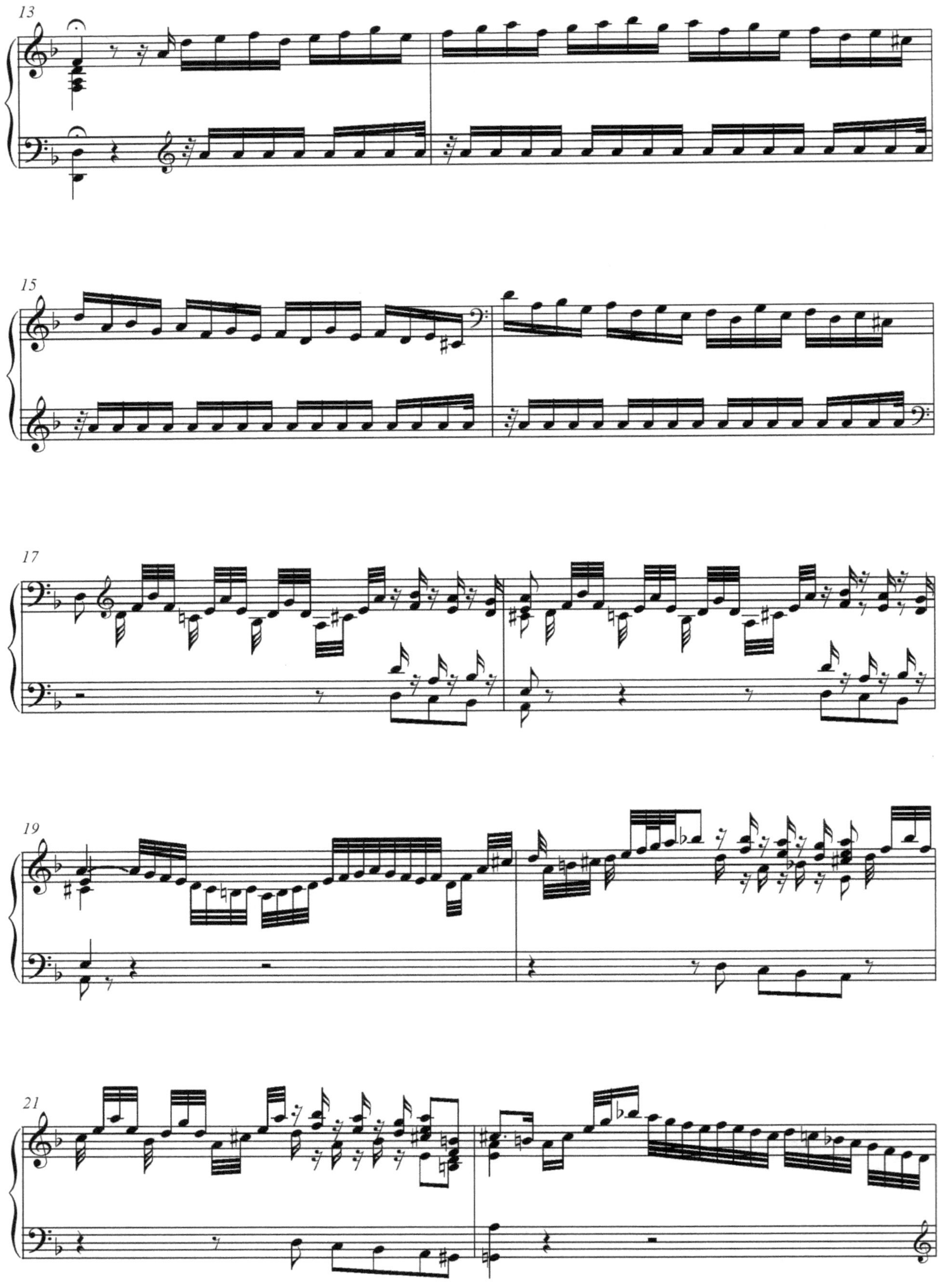
13
15
17
19
21

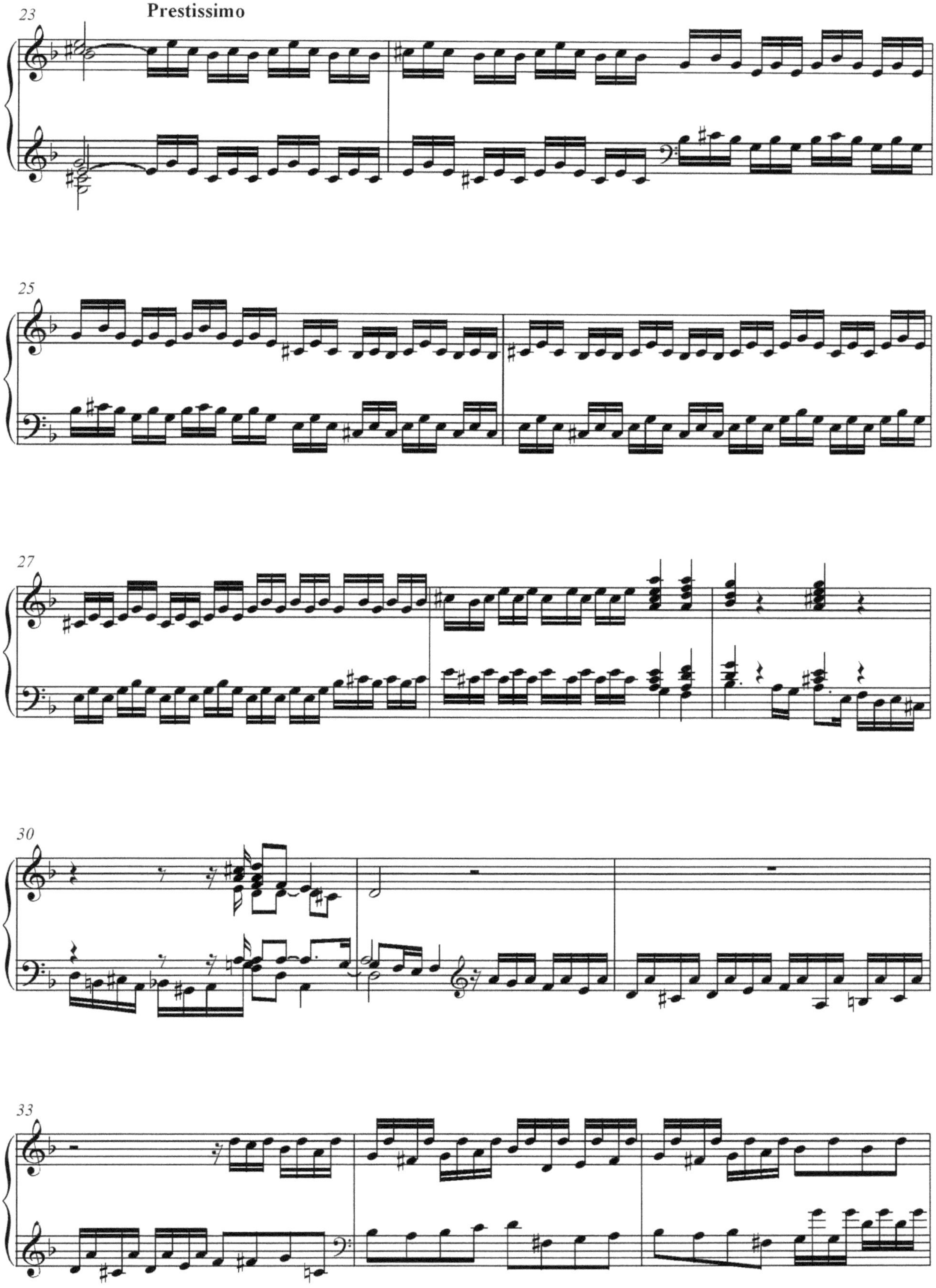
23
Prestissimo
25
27
30
33

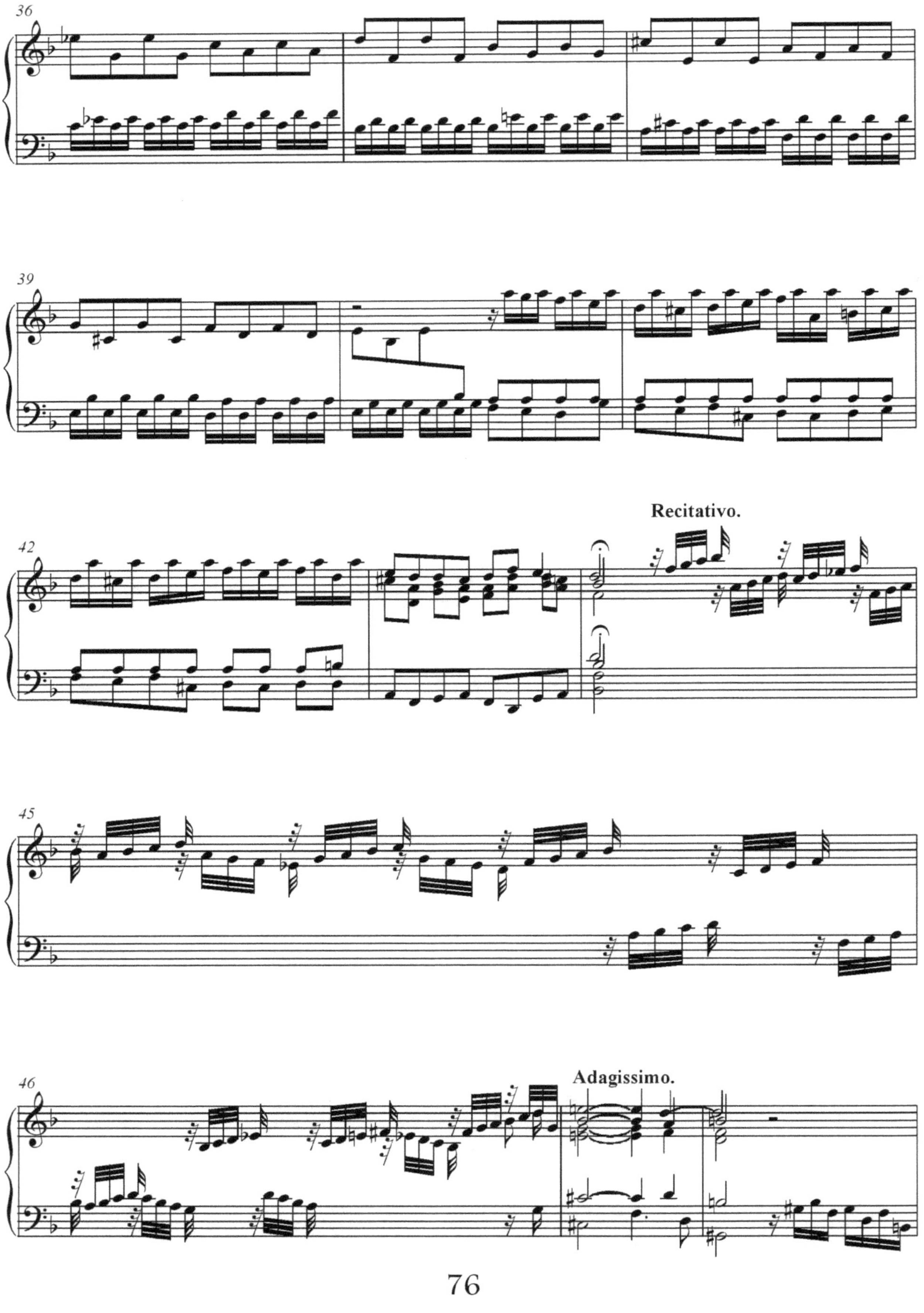
36
39
Recitativo.
42
45
Adagissimo.
46

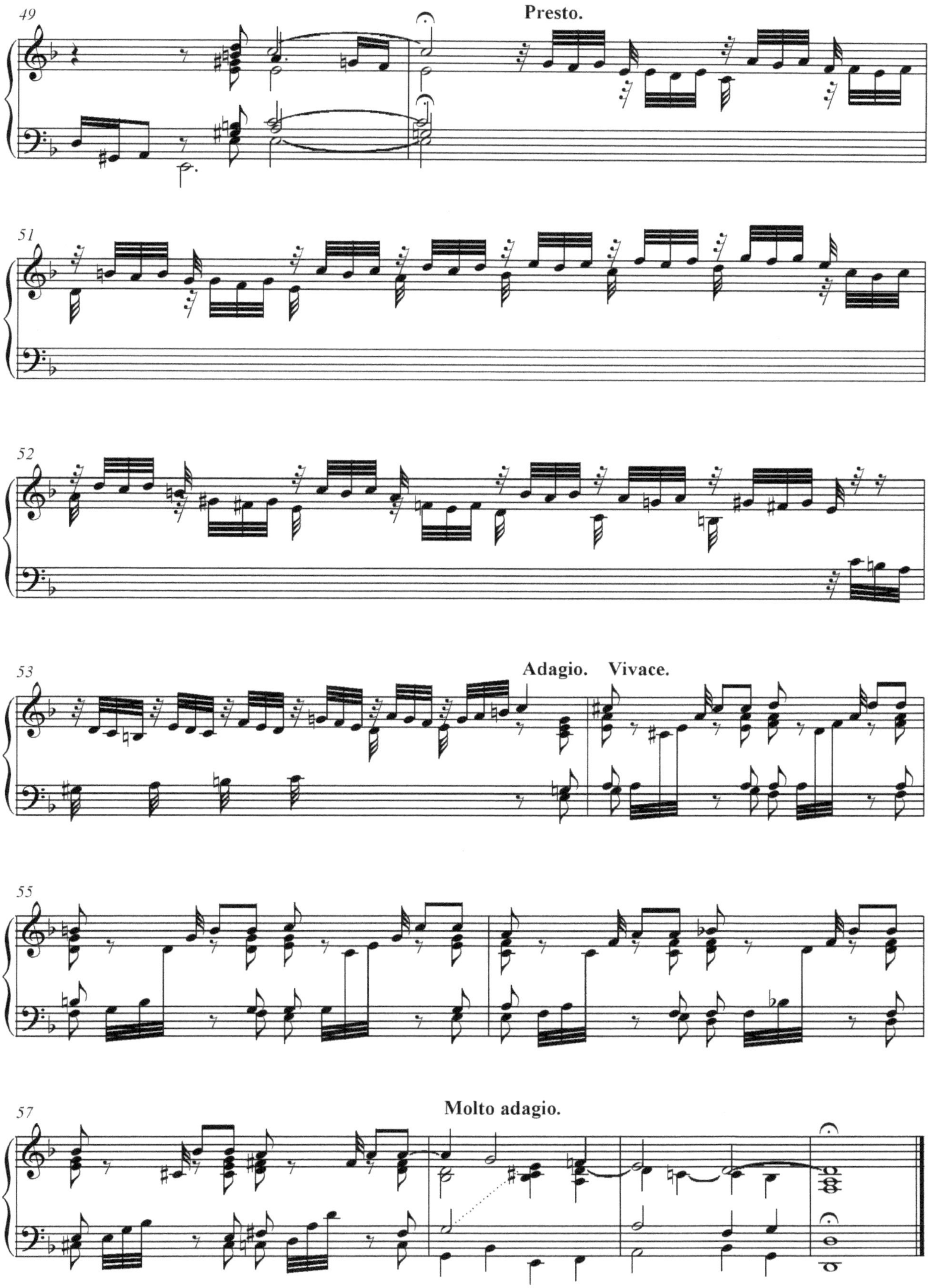
49
Presto.
51
52
53
Adagio.
Vivace.
55
57
Molto adagio.

Sonata in A minor
D.845

Franz Peter Schubert
Op.42

fp
f
cresc.
f
fz
p
fz
p
cresc.
ff
p
pp
molto espress.
mf
cresc.
f
p
pp
f
p
pp
dim.

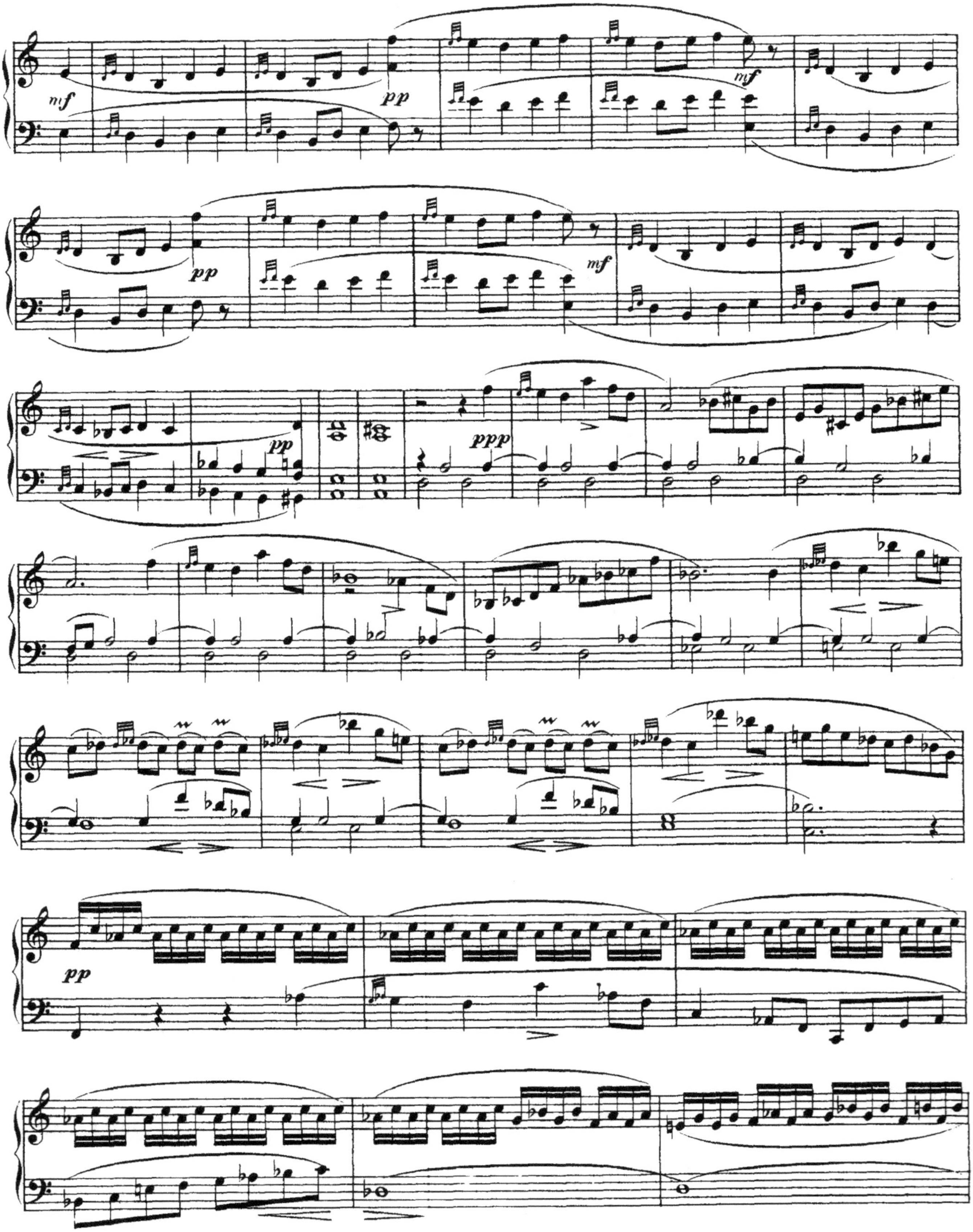
mf
pp
mf
pp
mf
pp
ppp
pp

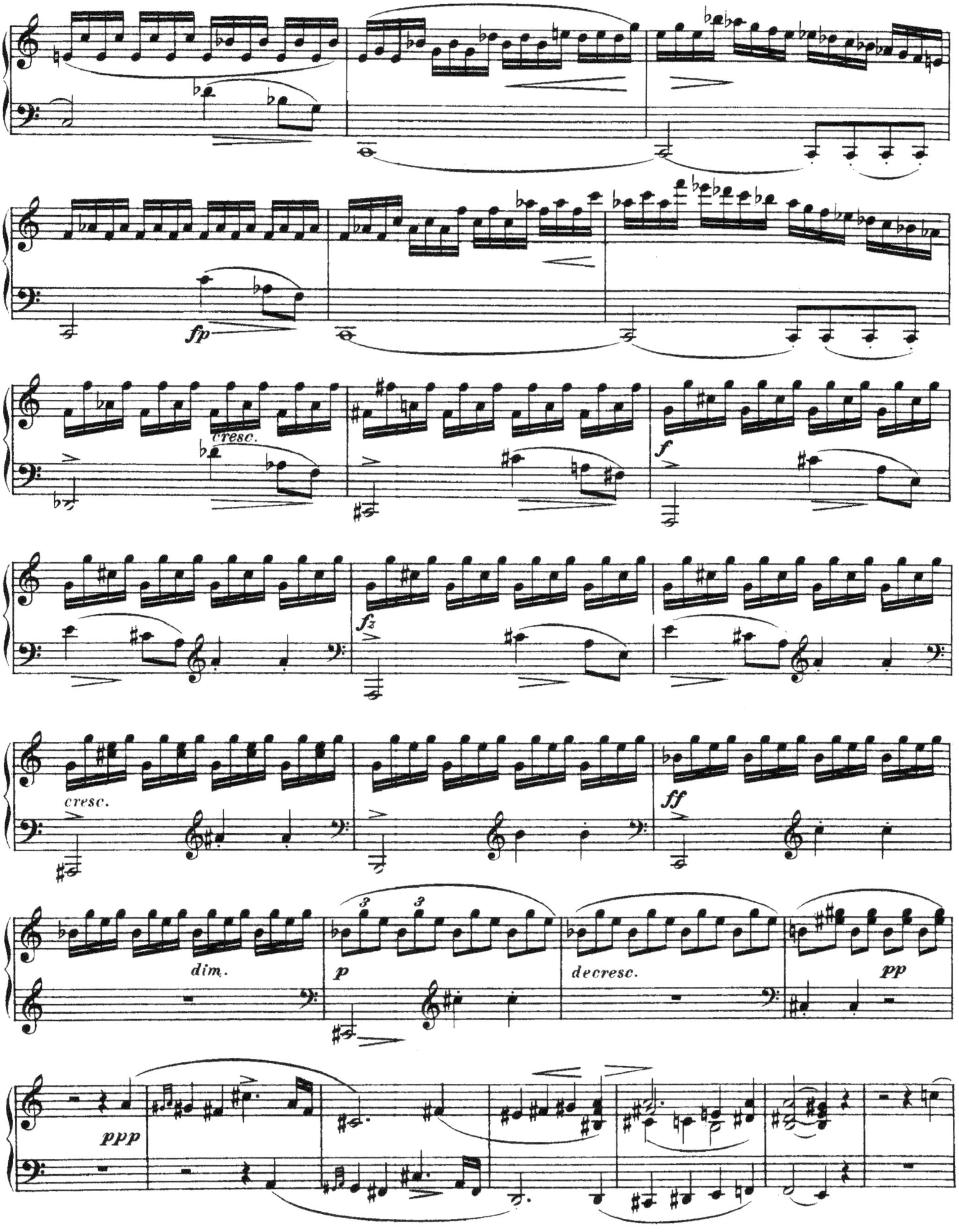
fp
cresc.
f
fz
cresc.
ff
dim.
p
decresc.
pp
ppp

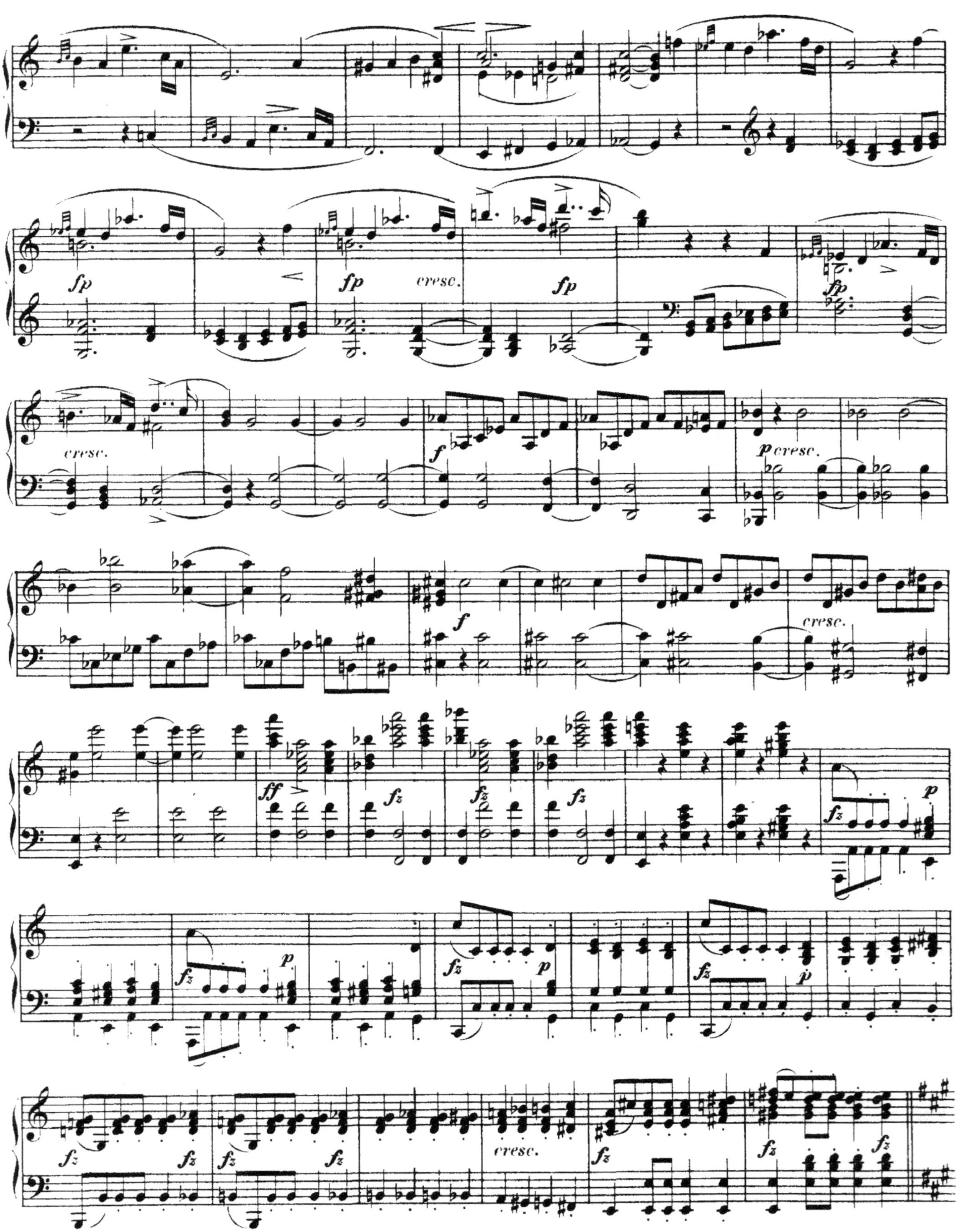
fp
cresc.
fp
cresc.
f
p cresc.
cresc.
ff
fz
p
cresc.

fp
cresc.
f
fp
cresc.
f
fz
p
fz
p
fz
ff
p
pp
pp
f
molto espress.
p
pp
f
pp
pp

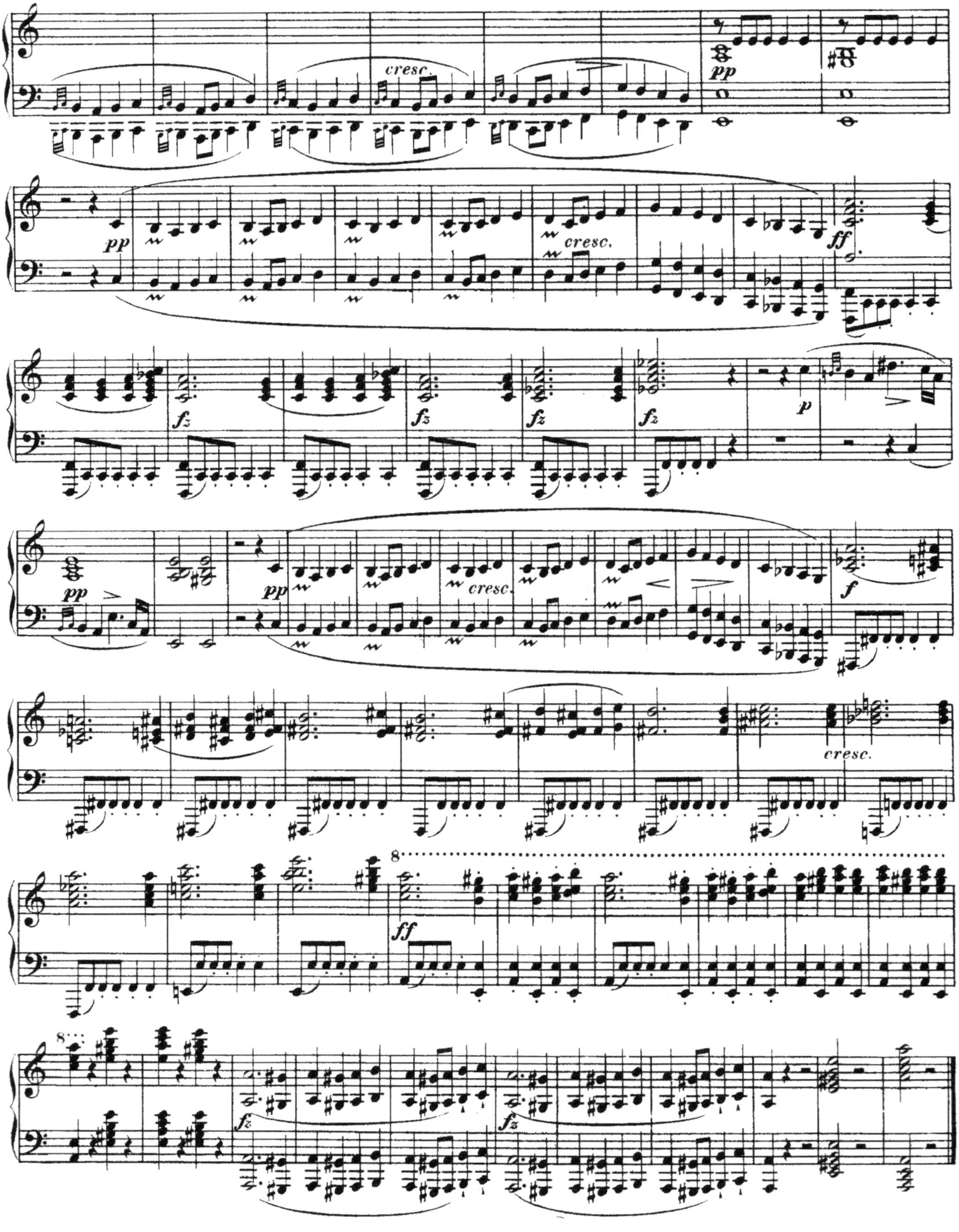

cresc.
pp
pp
cresc.
ff
fz
fz
fz
fz
p
pp
pp
cresc.
f
cresc.
8
ff
8
fz
fz

www.ingramcontent.com/pod-product-compliance
Lightning Source LLC
LaVergne TN
LVHW081348060426
835508LV00017B/1473